323.042 R888m
Roychoudhuri, Onnesha,
The marginalized majority :claiming
our power in a post-truth America

THE
MARGINALIZED
MAJORITY

CLAIMING OUR POWER IN

A POST-TRUTH AMERICA

Onnesha Roychoudhuri

 MELVILLE HOUSE

BROOKLYN

LONDON

The Marginalized Majority
Copyright © 2018 Onnesha Roychoudhuri
First Melville House printing: July 2018

Melville House Publishing
46 John Street
Brooklyn, NY 11201
and
Melville House UK
Suite 2000
16/18 Woodford Road
London E7 0HA

Design by Richard Oriolo

mhpbooks.com
facebook.com/mhpbooks
@melvillehouse

ISBN: 978-1-61219-699-2
ISBN: 978-1-61219-700-5 (eBook)

Printed in the United States of America

10 9 8 7 6 5 4 3 2 1

A catalog record for this book is available from the Library of Congress

TO THE POWERFUL MOVEMENT WE ALREADY ARE;

TO THE UNSTOPPABLE MOVEMENT WE'RE BECOMING

Somewhere we must come to see that human progress never rolls in on the wheels of inevitability. It comes through the tireless efforts and the persistent work of dedicated individuals who are willing to be co-workers with God. And without this hard work, time itself becomes an ally of the primitive forces of social stagnation. So we must help time and realize that the time is always ripe to do right.

—MARTIN LUTHER KING, JR.[1]

CONTENTS

THE MARGINALIZED MAJORITY

INTRODUCTION

We have frequently printed the word Democracy.

Yet I cannot too often repeat that it is a word the real

gist of which still sleeps, quite unawaken'd . . . It is a great

word, whose history, I suppose, remains unwritten,

because that history has yet to be enacted.

—*WALT WHITMAN*, DEMOCRATIC VISTAS[1]

E PLURIBUS PLURIBUS

DURING A RECENT VISIT WITH my mother, I sat flipping through an old photo album I'd never seen before. Inside were images of our extended family on my mother's side, stretching back to the time I was about four years old. My mother sat close to me, leaning in to offer captions as I turned the pages. I was laughing at the way I could chart the march of adolescence by my increasingly less amused facial expressions. As my cheeks began to grow more slender, the open smile transformed, offering up a paltry, tight-lipped semblance instead.

Toward the end of the album was an image that startled me: my mother and I sitting around a large table at a restaurant, most of her side of the family arranged in seats, beaming at the camera. My face, the only brown one at the table, stands out for another reason: I'm not even attempting a smile. In fact, I look furious. I noticed that my mother, who had been eagerly narrating the who, what, and where of each image, had gone silent. When I turned to look at her, she said simply, "Oh." "What?" I asked. My mother looked uncomfortable. "Well," she said, "if you don't remember, maybe it's better that way." This, of course, only piqued my curiosity. "Tell me," I said. My mother sighed. The dinner was to celebrate her parents' wedding anniversary; my uncle had just finished going around the table with his video camera in hand, naming everyone at the table. Except he had skipped over us.

Here was a historical moment I had forgotten until it resurfaced.

Uncle Bill didn't "believe in mixed marriage." Growing up, if I ever found myself in the same room or around the same dinner table as him, I could rely on one thing: He would not acknowledge my existence. He did not look at me and he did not speak to me. My general response was to simply ignore Bill the way he ignored me, though it would take me years before I could articulate how there was a power differential at play: He ignored me because my existence challenged his sensibilities. I ignored him because his sensibilities challenged my existence.

In retrospect, I'm grateful for the experience of growing up around my uncle Bill. Encountering racism and its tolerance in my own family gave me a model for what it means to grow up in America.

Of course, I did not have this outlook when I was a child. The situation felt like a private matter. I didn't tell my friends about the uncle who did not speak to me. I did not ask my mother questions about what it meant. Before I found my way to placing this experience in a broader framework of the institutional racism at the heart of this country's founding, it was a personal, even shameful, story to hold. I didn't want to look at it any more closely because I feared that if I scratched the surface, what I would come away with were concrete reasons why I was less worthy of acknowledgment, of acceptance—even of existence—in this country.

THESE QUESTIONS OF WHO *belongs* and who doesn't, who is a person worth counting and who isn't, have always preoccupied us in America. There's the early stuff of our country's founding—the "handful" of "uncivilized" and "intractable" natives who populated the country before Europeans landed on its shores, offering the gifts of these preposterously off-base adjectives along with smallpox and influenza plagues. When those indigenous people died en masse from those plagues, as well as deliberate slaughter, the African slave trade filled the gap—men, women, and children shackled and shipped over to the New World to provide a new form of free labor to sustain the country's economy. Then there were the waves of willing immigrants who arrived seeking a better life. With so many cultures and languages colliding on America's shores, there has always been tension, and the attendant question of whether being American means to scrub yourself of your particularities, or to celebrate them.

We learn about the fractioning of human beings in a section of our high school history textbooks: each slave counting as three-fifths of a person for the purposes of getting slave owners more representation in Congress. We're encouraged to read these historical narratives as static, safely ensconced in the container of the past, where they ostensibly remain without leaking. We're encouraged to think of *ourselves* as outside of that history, too—here to study it rather than participate in the making of it. The narrative, say, of our country overturning Jim Crow, comes to us framed in a tone of inevitability. *Of course* we had to do away with these unfair laws, the logic of these few glossy pages in our history books implies, *it was just a matter of time.*

There's something tricky in the definition of "history" as we commonly use it—the study of past events. Viewed in this way, history ruptures continuity, severing itself from the present and future. Maybe there is a kind of American-hued wish at the heart of this understanding of history—to not be lashed to the past, to invent ourselves anew. But, of course, this severance is impossible.

The word "history" comes from the Greek *historia*, meaning "knowledge acquired by investigation." There's more promise in this etymology—room for engagement and continuity. We are accustomed to thinking of the future as containing unknowns. But the past, too, is full of hidden and lesser-known narratives. What might these narratives tell us about who we are and what's possible?

How does it change our understanding of the United States, for instance, to acknowledge that contemporary estimates of indigenous peoples in the Americas put the population at roughly 50–100 million people in the late 1400s before they were decimated by European diseases—ten times that of earlier estimates?[2] Or that many of these indigenous civilizations were far more advanced in agriculture, architecture, and mathematics than the early British and Spanish empires?[3] How does it change our understanding of our country to learn that the US Constitution was modeled on the Iroquois Confederacy? Or that, by 1860, the United States counted 4 million slaves among its population, valued at a worth of $3.5 billion—making them, as historian David Blight points out, the largest financial asset in the US economy, worth more than all railroads and manufacturing *combined?*[4]

What do these narratives tell us about whose country this is?

WE ARE MANY. WE ARE ONE. The copper two-cent coin was first issued in 1864, and it was conspicuously missing the usual motto: *E pluribus unum*—"out of many, one." The Civil War was in its third year, and it seemed impossible to agree on who were the many, and who were the one. Fast forward to 1938, when the House Un-American Activities Committee was created to investigate whether any Americans had communist ties, which, according to the committee's calculus, would make them un-American. Fast forward even further to 2008, when, just days before the presidential election, Minnesota Republican representative Michele Bachmann accused Barack Obama and other congressional Democrats of harboring "anti-American views," and suggested that the media investigate possible "un-American" activities.[5]

During the 2008 campaign, vice presidential candidate Sarah Palin referred repeatedly to "real America," which was apparently located only in small, rural areas of the country. Shows like *Saturday Night Live*, *The Colbert Report*, and *The Daily Show* all parodied the rise of public figures like Palin and Bachmann. We laughed along with a fringe-wigged Tina Fey as she repeated lines from Palin's media appearances almost verbatim, raising the question of what purpose satire serves in our contemporary political era. What we understood was that when Tina Fey repeated what Palin said, Fey didn't mean what she was saying. This restored a sense of sanity to those of us who could not, or did not want to believe that people like Palin and Bachmann could represent America. We laughed along knowingly, cynically, but above all, dismissively. These people were ridiculous—what was happening in the country was ridiculous—and we sought solace by feeling somehow separate from and unsullied by it all.

Thankfully, we were granted a reprieve. This appeal to the narrative of division—separating the "real" from the "fake," the "American" from the "un-American" didn't take. Barack Obama won the election in a landslide victory, insisting on an America of inclusion. As cynical and detached as many of us had grown after eight years of the Bush administration and the launch of a seemingly endless global "war on terror," Obama appealed to us on remarkably earnest grounds with rallying cries of "Yes we can" and "Hope" throughout his campaign.

At his victory rally, facing a throng of hundreds of thousands of supporters at Grant Park in Chicago, Obama reiterated his message of inclusion, noting that his election was "the answer spoken by young and old, rich and poor, Democrat and Republican, black, white, Hispanic, Asian, Native American, gay, straight, disabled and not disabled. Americans who sent a message to the world that we have never been just a collection of individuals or a collection of red states and blue states. We are, and always will be, the United States of America."[6]

What to make of a man whose Americanness had been called into question now suddenly holding the highest office of the land? In his concession speech, John McCain told his supporters: "America today is a world away from the cruel and frightful bigotry of that time. There is no better evidence of this than the election of an African American to the presidency of the United States."

Only this widely circulated quote comes from a high-gloss

transcript, doing away with the intriguing trips and stumbles found in public speeches. What McCain actually said was: "There is no better evidence of this than the election of an Ameri . . . an African American to the presidency." For a moment, these two terms, "American" and "African American," charged with static, vied for prominence.[7]

What might have happened if McCain and Palin had won the election? It was a question I did not think about. Democracy had proven itself. America had proven itself. I suddenly, proudly, stood behind both of those tricky and malleable terms as though they had finally delivered on their promises. I, like the other 69.5 million Americans who had voted for Obama (the highest number of votes ever won by a president,[8] 43 percent of which came from white voters),[9] was in shock that the election had so swiftly been won. And by a *black man* no less.

I was living in San Francisco at the time, working as a journalist. I had hunkered down in a friend's apartment to watch the returns roll in. We were prepared for a long night, so when Obama was declared the winner at 8 p.m., we didn't know quite what to do with ourselves. We heard cheering nearby and walked outside the apartment building to see a few other folks doing the same. We all looked up Valencia Street, where the ruckus was coming from, and went toward it.

I have yet to experience another spontaneous public celebration like the one that occurred on the evening of November 4, 2008, in San Francisco. Thousands of people gathered in the streets, popping champagne and malt liquor bottles, passing them to strangers and friends alike. A man shimmied to the top of a traffic light while police looked on, unamused yet untroubled.

People came pouring out of cars onto side streets, where they had pulled over once they realized they couldn't go any farther. They, too, seemed untroubled as members of the crowd continued to pass bottles and kiss cheeks with the relish of elderly aunts. I drank deep—of the moment and of the booze.

After years of covering the George W. Bush administration as a journalist, I was exhausted. Every day had felt like a game of catch-up to whatever the latest administration run-around was—watching a slow and steady erosion of civil liberties in the wake of 9/11, the mire of the Iraq War and the administration's lies that led us into it, the burgeoning "war on terror" that followed. It was a full-time job simply keeping up with whatever new gap in reality—between what the administration was purporting and what reporters were unearthing—emerged on any given day.

Throughout the Bush administration, I watched as White House spokespeople denied facts published on the front pages of every major paper. It felt like a clear refusal to acknowledge reality—a strategy I was deeply troubled to see confirmed when journalist Ron Suskind published a story citing what a Bush aide (later revealed to be Karl Rove) had told him in 2004:

> [W]hen we act, we create our own reality. And while you're studying that reality—judicially as you will—we'll act again, creating other new realities, which you can study, too, and that's how things will sort out. We're history's actors . . . and you, all of you, will be left to just study what we do.[10]

If those in power were banking on our complacency, if they were so cynically disdainful of reality itself, what hope was there for the rest of us?

I no longer believed my reporting would change anything. Instead, I merely hoped that when it was all over, it might serve as a trail of bread crumbs—a way to find our way back to a shared reality, to the privileges and liberties we used to enjoy, the aspirational principles of equality and inclusivity our leadership used to at least pay lip service to.

Obama's election—his earnest appeal to those values of equality, inclusivity, and his respect for facts and a shared reality—was the first time I and so many others had felt genuine hope in years. It felt like a collective sigh of relief. Marching up Valencia Street that night, I was celebrating what felt like a collective moment in which we on the Left were flirting with becoming true believers of some kind, and maybe even that rare beast among those of us well acquainted with the darker side of our history—proud Americans.

LIKE SO MANY OTHER Americans, I let Obama's election serve as a balm. Over the next eight years, I became more complacent, more trusting of those in power. My guy had won, so I could sit and enjoy the victory. (Right?) I could trust that those executive powers that had continued to expand in scope over the past five decades and gave the president unprecedented unchecked power, were probably in trustworthy hands.[11] (Right?) I still followed the news, I still sometimes wrote the news, but I started branching out, writing more fiction and essays, feeling a freedom to explore what else I might have to say now that I didn't have to spend so much energy trying to bridge the gap between the administration's reality and my own. A part of me felt like my work was done: I had helped elect a progressive, black president who had vowed to fight to improve the quality of life for *all* Americans.

But history cannot be severed from the present moment.

Fast forward to 2016, when Donald Trump—who, between the years of 2011 and 2014 repeatedly questioned whether Obama was born in the United States—was named the president-elect.[12] Also, there's this: for thirteen years, one of Trump's closest mentors was Roy Cohn—Senator Joseph McCarthy's lawyer during the communist witch hunt that was made manifest in the House Un-American Activities Committee.[13]

Which is to say: This narrative of the "un-American" has always been in the present. Right alongside the narrative of America and democracy as shorthand for the promises of equality and inclusivity. Right alongside those of us who would—with a countervailing cynicism—count ourselves apart, sitting at home, mainlining episodes of late-night comedy, laughing half-heartedly at a country and leadership we refused to take responsibility for.

THE NIGHT OF THE 2016 election there was a different kind of shock. A few friends gathered at a bar. This time, we expect the results to come in quickly, and they do. Only it's not what we've been told to expect. A man standing next to me, our faces angled toward the TV, turns and looks searchingly in my face. "You know, when I'm feeling anxious, I find deep breathing to be really helpful." He begins to demonstrate for me, his hand on his diaphragm, and I stifle a sudden, violent impulse. As the minutes and then hours begin to wear on, people filter out of the bar, confident they've seen enough. I stay. I have the wherewithal to keep it together until I get my key in the front door of my apartment, and finally allow the tears of fear and outrage I'd held back throughout the night.

A man who bragged about grabbing a woman by the pussy, accused a judge of having a conflict of interest because he had Mexican heritage, mocked a reporter's disability, was going to be sitting in the White House. It's not that I didn't believe it could happen. It's that I was terrified of what was to come.

I was not wrong to be terrified. Within a few weeks of the election, there was a disturbing uptick in hate crimes across the country.[14] Even in New York City. At neighborhood playgrounds were newly spray-painted swastikas, Muslims punched on park benches in Queens—one of the most diverse regions on the planet. An Asian man on a train was beaten and told to "go back to your country."

Just days after his victory, Trump appoints Steve Bannon—who boasted about his publication Breitbart becoming the platform for the "alt-right"—his chief strategist. From a hotel conference room in Washington, neo-Nazi ("alt-right") leader Richard Spencer delivers a "Hail, Trump" speech during which audience members cheered him on with Nazi salutes. "It's not just that [the mainstream media] are leftists and cucks," Spencer intones into his microphone. "It's not just that many are genuinely stupid. Indeed, one wonders if these people are people at all."

The audience laughs.[15]

I know it should not be surprising when certain narratives that have been part of America since its founding bubble up to the surface. But still.

Two weeks after the election, I ended up at a friend's Thanksgiving gathering in Brooklyn. When I made my way back to the dinner table after a trip to the bathroom, I had traveled through a porthole to a previous decade.

"You're just in time," a woman told me. I hadn't retained her name, only the details: recently relocated from Tampa, Florida; thin, bright lipstick. The rest of my dinner companions had been living in New York for years, a group of primarily young white men. Around the table, the men fell silent, a rare occurrence since

I'd arrived. "We're debating," Tampa explained, "whether women are funny."

"Whether women are *as funny* as men," one of the men qualified graciously.

I felt my heart quicken. "Why don't we just debate," I suggested, smiling, not wanting to let my agitation be seen, "whether women are people at all." My voice betrayed my rage.

It had begun. The emboldening of bigots and bigotry that trickled into every stratum of our social and political lives, revealing a frightening and uncertain atmosphere, one in which the terms of debates and the terms of reality—whether they be around dinner tables or in the halls of Congress—are up for grabs.

The intensity of the fears I had during the Bush years flooded my system all over again. Where White House officials under Bush were cagey toward the press, Trump declared a wholesale war on journalists, tweeting that the press was the "enemy of the people."[16] Sexual assault became "locker-room talk." Racism became a bold refusal to cower to "political correctness." Neo-Nazis became the "alt-right." We were moving from the George W. era of "truthiness" to the Trump era of "alternative facts." In other words—from some frayed cord still connected to the truth to an utter rending of that cord.

I WAS ALSO DEEPLY afraid of a return to the disaffection and cynicism that had grown rampant during the two terms of George W. Bush's presidency. "Not my president," became a rallying cry after Trump's election—a sentiment that captured what many of us were feeling, but one that also raised the question of who *did* have power.

The question on the lips of so many in the days after the election was, *What now?* Those of us who put our politics on the back burner during the previous eight years looked to those we had surrendered our hope to for answers.

What we got was Hillary Clinton's heartfelt concession speech. "I still believe in America, and I always will," she concluded. "And if you do, then we must accept this result and then look to the future. Donald Trump is going to be our president. We owe him an open mind and the chance to lead."[17]

A few hours later, President Obama echoed this language of duty and obligation: "[W]e are now all rooting for his success in uniting and leading the country. The peaceful transition of power is one of the hallmarks of our democracy. And over the next few months, we are going to show that to the world."[18]

The message struck me, on a core level, as all wrong. How was it my patriotic obligation to legitimate the power of a man who had continually expressed contempt for mine? Accepting that the election of a man who campaigned on the basis of exclusion, bigotry, and sexism was democracy at work constituted a kind of moral acrobatics I was not limber enough for.

So many of us were experiencing a deep disbelief, and beneath it was this question: How, as a country, did we go from electing someone like Barack Obama to electing someone like Donald Trump?

Despite a growing shift to the left in Americans' beliefs on issues ranging from support of gay marriage to single-payer health insurance, the platforms of Democratic political leadership remain quite a few steps behind, while those of Republicans are blatantly out of step.[19] This dissonance is nothing new: in the late Reagan years, for instance, 70 percent of Americans thought there should be a constitutional guarantee of health care, despite the fact that Reagan railed against "socialized medicine for every

American."[20] For decades, political scientists like Walter Dean Burnham have pointed to the absence of a robust political party that represents the interests of everyday Americans as a primary reason so many choose to sit elections out. For Burnham, that means the absence of a thriving laborite or socialist party, the latter of which had historically represented the interests of a cross section of the labor, peace, civil rights, and civil liberties movements. The decline in unions—which have historically advocated for workers' rights and often worked as a powerful organizing force for Democratic candidates—plays a part in this alienation, too. While unions were key to the victories of Democratic presidents like Bill Clinton and Barack Obama, both failed to pass robust labor-law reforms to strengthen unions. In less than 40 years (from 1978 to 2017) union membership has fallen from 26 to 10.7 percent.[21] Perhaps Americans choose not to vote because they no longer recognize their interests in either remaining party platform.

What if the Democratic and Republican parties have moved so far to the right—away from the concerns of the vast majority of Americans—that to call the two-party system as it stands a democracy is *itself* anti-democratic? Keep in mind, too, that 42 percent of eligible American voters chose not to vote in the 2016 election—a nod to the fact that a real choice made by many Americans was "none of the above."[22]

In the wake of the election, a story emerged—headlines breathlessly lamented how polarized the country had become. This narrative has been recycled over and over in op-eds and think pieces, reflected in new polls, numbers that try to quantify how much it is we cannot stand each other, have no common ground, live in "different" Americas.

But it also remains true that we saw a twist in the lead up to the 2016 election: Bernie Sanders, a candidate whose campaign relied solely on grassroots funders, and Donald Trump, a candidate whose wealth was advertised as a hallmark of his independence from the "swamp" of Washington. The popularity of both spoke of voters' desire for something different. Perhaps, too, it spoke to some understanding that corporate interests and party funding have run amok. Why does this narrative seem less available or convincing to us than "Americans have grown unprecedentedly polarized"?

The more closely I examined the dissonance behind the turn our country seemed to take in this election, the clearer it became that we're lacking an instructive narrative that reflects the reality we're in: The majority of Americans voted for a Democrat.[23] For at least the past fifteen years, Americans have continued to express increasingly liberal values and beliefs.[24] Since 2011, there have been waves of social movements, many following on the heels of Occupy Wall Street, that have gained power and visibility: from racial-justice movements like Black Lives Matter, to immigrant-rights movements like the DREAMers, to climate-justice movements like the Climate Justice Alliance. That many of these movements have successfully collaborated and organized together counters another story we're often told: that protest is ineffectual, that the progressive movement is too fractured, too consumed with "identity politics" to be a broadly mobilizing force.

The ranks of people concerned enough to take a stand have grown: in the days after the election, millions flooded the streets in the United States and around the world to let it be known that they stand against bigotry, misogyny, and exclusionary policies. It is into *this* landscape that Trump has entered.

What if, instead of viewing this as a country divided, we view it as a country in a political moment when we do not have the leadership the majority of us want and deserve? The narrative chasm is of a different sort—not between Americans themselves, but between Americans and the political leadership that no longer represents them.

TRAVELING THROUGH MY HOMETOWN in North Carolina in the days after the Women's March in Washington, D.C., I ran into an old friend getting a drink at a bar I used to frequent. He was there with a colleague of his—a fellow high school teacher. The conversation turned to politics pretty quickly, and the friend, B., adamantly put forth the notion that there was nothing to be done except wait out the next four awful years. Look at the numbers in Congress, he said. Look at the Supreme Court. *We're all fucked.*

For those of us who checked out after Obama was elected, it can be tempting to do the same now. This, too, is something I fear—that progressives will once again be pushed back on our heels, responding to those in power with, at worst, our heads in the sand, and at best, a robust "no." Too often in this process of saying no, we lose sight of—and energy for—the work of making demands, recognizing our own power, insisting on the reality we live in, and the reality we must work toward.

B. and I began to hash it out. In his mind, he was being realistic, practical, pragmatic. From my perspective, he was being profoundly cynical, and making an argument that flew in the face of history. What about the millions of people around the world who took to the streets on the day after Donald Trump's inauguration? What about the ever-leftward-moving views of Americans—particularly among the younger generation that would soon be of voting age?[25] What about the growth of progressive movements over the past decade, the likes of which we haven't seen since the civil rights era?

The majority of us inhabit a reality that exists parallel to Trump's. I told B. that if we buy into the cynicism that there is nothing to be done, we lose sight of the world we already live in. We let the Roves and Trumps of the world dictate reality. After decades of progressive momentum, we've reached an important juncture where we either surrender our narrative, our reality, to those in power, or hold fast and push forward. To choose now as the moment in which we give in to cynicism and say, *What's the point?*, is to throw into the fire the history books of a future generation—the ones that might tell the story of how Americans seized democracy from the clutches of an elite handful of cynical, opportunistic oligarchs.

The stakes have never been higher: Every day brings new initiatives aimed at turning back the clock, consolidating wealth in the hands of the 1 percent, slashing access to medical care and education, removing protections for the most marginalized among us. Many of us are experiencing a shift in our perception of time because of the intensity and trauma of a leadership that shocks us daily—a single day can feel like a week, a week can feel like a month. News curation projects like "What the Fuck Just Happened Today"—an email digest, billing itself as "[t]oday's essential guide to the daily shock and awe in national politics"—have cropped up in direct response to the barrage of Trump-related headlines emerging every day.

There are now countless opportunities for action, but that also means more opportunities to feel hopeless and disempowered. If we don't reframe our relationship to our own power and recognize the vital role we must play now, we sacrifice our current challenging reality to one that may become unsurvivable.

Now is the time for us to set the terms of the conversation, to push back with the reality we insist on.

About an hour and a couple of drinks later, B. was still unconvinced and I was still deeply frustrated. It seemed to me that he was funneling energy that could be used to fight for the reality he wanted into defending his choice to *not* do anything. He was weaving a narrative about how powerless we were, one that echoed Rove's "history's actors" quote perfectly. This is why the cynical narrative is so dangerous: it can be much easier to believe there's nothing we can do. Hope and action are dangerous things—they speak of time, effort, investment, of giving a shit, of potential failure. For too long, hope has been associated with a kind of humorless, dewy-eyed naïveté. But look back on the civil rights era: Who would argue that those fighting to end Jim Crow laws were naive? Hope is only naive when it's divorced from action and investment. With those forces in play, it becomes a revolutionary muscle.

Hope is the thing that makes us try, that makes us human, that makes us consciously evolve. It is what sustains long-term vision—something many of us too easily relinquish in the face of opposition. As LGBTQ activist Rea Carey entreated in the wake of Trump's election: "Just take a few seconds and imagine a world where we are truly free, where *you* are truly free. What will that feel like?"[26]

Without a vision to fight for, we relegate ourselves to a paralyzing narrative that serves as a straitjacket for the majority of Americans. At best, that narrative keeps us bound by inequality; at worst, it kills us. Hope is about staying in the fight, it's about survival. Understood in this light, we realize that hope is not some indulgence, it is practical and pragmatic. In short: there is no other option.

Two days after our conversation, I received a message from B., referencing an interview I had recently published at *Rolling Stone* about the history and power of protest: "Our conversation has been on my mind, and after reading your article I see how deeply engaged you are in trying to take positive action during this dreary time. I'm really trying to rally, and felt more than a touch ashamed of my wearying cynicism. So, for what it's worth, thank you."[27] It was a message I did not expect, and it was one that encouraged me to dig further, to examine the narratives that have led me and so many others to count ourselves out or sit on the sidelines.

IT WAS MY UNCLE Bill who I was thinking of when, one day recently in Brooklyn, a man boarded my subway train and let loose an impassioned and bigoted tirade. My fellow New Yorkers did their job of ignoring him admirably, but he didn't keep up his end of the bargain, which was to move on after a few stops and pester the next car down.

After fifteen minutes straight of his proselytizing, some passengers told him to shut up. He wouldn't. Some tried reasoning with him. But here's the thing about narcissistic ideologues: they don't respond to logic, or dissuasion in the name of facts or reason. We could fact-check him all day and night, but he wasn't playing by the rules of the game.

In that moment, I wrestled with a familiar feeling of resignation and powerlessness. I closed my eyes in the stuffy train and thought to myself: *It'll be over soon.* But I was tired of allowing the loudest and most bombastic among us to take control by default.

I decided that if the man would not shut up, the only way to improve the situation would be to make it so we no longer had to listen to him. I told him that if he wouldn't stop talking, I would start singing so that I'd no longer have to hear him.

He kept talking. So I sang.

The first round of "Row, Row, Row Your Boat" was shaky and a little off-key. It was all I could muster. But a few people joined in the next round, and by the third, everyone on the train was singing robustly—including a couple kids in strollers who clapped their hands in glee. The proselytizer tried to get loud, but we got louder. Suddenly, we were no longer the audience for a hateful man. He got off at the next stop, yet we kept singing a few more rounds, smiling at each other and enjoying the simple joy of the reality and world that we'd reclaimed.

I KNOW WE CANNOT simply sing Trump off the train. But I wonder at the strategic uses of ignoring the loudest bigot on the train by turning our attention and intentions toward each other—the quieter majority. I wonder at the strategic uses of denial and disbelief—that privilege I've occassionally allowed myself in order to feel more free as a brown woman to say and think what I please, to not police myself with the expectations of bigots and buffoons. I think about the lunch counter sit-ins during the civil rights era. How at the heart of the strategy was a refusal to accept unjust laws and policies. To strategically ignore the rules and insist on a different world: one in which black men and women could sit and eat at the same counter as any other human being.

I want to take this principle and apply it more broadly. How can we actively, strategically, ignore Donald Trump?

A part of that answer lies in recognizing the power we already have and counting ourselves in rather than sitting on the sidelines, only explicitly acknowledging that we're American when, say, checking the citizenship box on official paperwork.

History is happening now and we are history's actors. But only if we can turn our attention to each other, acknowledge the power we have, and step up to own it. There are millions of us who are fighting for the same things—and millions more who want the same things but call them by a different name. Yet we still seem to struggle to understand ourselves as a movement, we struggle to recognize and take responsibility for how powerful we are. The shape of our potential remains a dotted line describing the parameters of something we're hesitant to inhabit and lay claim to.

Part of this is about the anemic narratives on offer—about the marginalized, the ineffectual, and disorganized Left. For too long, we've accepted stories that disenfranchise us even when they fly in the face of facts, logic, and our shared reality. We have all come of age in a society that privileges white Americans—particularly straight, white, cisgender men. But this has become an increasingly odd dissonance with the reality of our population: only 31 percent of Americans today are white men—and some fraction of them are more marginalized queer and transgender men.[28]

The marginalized are now the majority, but our narratives around power haven't kept up. As long as we continue to operate within the strictures of outdated narratives, we sacrifice our ability to recognize the reality of our power, our ability to *produce* reality, to live in the world we want (and need). History is full of narratives that correct this perspective, but these stories have been forgotten or given short shrift in textbooks. Even when they are presented, too often they're shrouded in a tone of inevitability when the untold details speak of profound struggle and the necessity of "failed" efforts that preceded that "inevitable" turn.

What follows is an attempt to resurface stories that have gone missing, and to reckon with narratives that have been passed off as common sense when they're anything but. These problematic narratives include a deeply flawed connotation of "objectivity" that has come to be dominant in the media and daily life; the perceived divide between the personal and political; the ineffectiveness of protest; and, the conceit that we must always listen and respond to those in power. By holding these narratives up to the light, we see space for other possibilities. When we surface—and contribute—richer narratives, we see a different history and a different reality; one in which the stories of "marginalized" folks are, and always have been, at the heart of this country.

I wonder what kind of power we might find in recognizing the centrality of our stories.

ON CYNICISM

A man walks into a pub and hits a guy over the head with an
iron bar. The guy who got hit says, 'Was that serious
or a joke?' The guy says, 'It was serious.' The other
guy says, 'Thank god, I hate jokes like that.'

—*ERIC IDLE*, THE ARISTOCRATS[1]

When [Diogenes the Cynic] was sold as a slave, he endured
it most nobly . . . When the auctioneer asked in what
he was proficient, he replied, 'In ruling men.' Thereupon
he pointed to a certain Corinthian with a fine purple
border to his robe . . . and said, 'Sell me to this
man; he needs a master.'

—*DIOGENES LAERTIUS*, LIVES OF EMINENT PHILOSOPHERS[2]

HERE WE ARE

THE DAY AFTER DONALD TRUMP was sworn in as president of the United States, half a million people flooded the streets of Washington, D.C. I was there, scarf wrapped around my throat, a handful of cough drops wedged in the pocket of my jeans. I was sick, but I didn't want to miss the Women's March—the first large-scale action planned in the wake of the election. I've always hated crowds, but a combination of righteous fear, fury, and a nip of whiskey got me up to the task. There I was, shoulder-to-shoulder with a fierce array of chant-

ers and sign-holders—and that was just on the subway ride over
to the rally. The trains were so packed with people that it took
nearly two hours to get above ground. So many people crammed
into such a small space seemed like a recipe for short tempers,
but people were remarkably companionable—joining in cho-
ruses of "Lean On Me" while we waited for the subway doors to
open, leading call-and-response chants ("Hey hey, ho ho, Donald
Trump has got to go") as we moved slowly up the stairs leading
above ground.

The plan was for speakers like Angela Davis, Gloria Steinem,
and Michael Moore to address the crowd before we all marched.
I stood on Independence Avenue, growing antsy at the seemingly
endless roster of speakers whose words I could barely make out
through the PA system, waiting for the time that we could march.
But after the last speaker wrapped up, an announcement was
made that the route we were supposed to march was too crowded
with people. A disembodied voice notified us that, *We've already
accomplished what we set out to do.*

I scanned the crowd and my gaze fell on a young woman holding what looked like a cold slice of pizza in one hand and cradling
an "Impeachment Now" sign in the other.

It seemed unlikely that I was the only one who felt like we
hadn't yet accomplished what we'd set out to.

Millions of us had traveled from across the country. We
weren't just going to take our signs and go home after a few
hours of listening and milling around. We were unsure of the
future, full of a kind of anxious energy that we wanted to direct
somewhere. So we did. Instead of going home, the crowd started
moving toward the National Mall—slowly converging with other
offshoots of protests that had gathered in nearby streets. We continued marching—down Independence and Constitution Ave-
nues. Taking a right up 14th or 10th Streets brought another

discovery—some other throng of protesters, people packed as tightly in the streets as we had been in the subway cars that morning. At one point, I clambered atop a large concrete planter to get a better view of the crowds streaming through the streets, to have some sense of where it began and ended. All I could see were more people in more streets. We were everywhere.

The question of what we were or were not "accomplishing"— parsed over and over again by news and opinion pieces leading up to the protests—had quieted in my mind. I had wondered that, too, of course. Who were we all, and what did we all want? Like millions of other people in the United States and around the world, I felt a deep sense of panic after the election. I woke up and fell asleep with the question *What can we do?*, like a restless mantra, worrying my mind and tongue. But all of these questions were momentarily drowned out by the fact of what I was seeing: the size of the crowd, the volubility of us. As we marched through the streets, full of joy and outrage, it felt like we were cementing an obvious but vital recognition: *I see you. I see us.* After the shock of the election, the simple fact of so many of us being in the streets felt like a necessary salve.

This is the start of something, I thought. We're making history.

And we were. The Women's March was the largest single-day protest in US history. D.C. had been expecting two hundred thousand people, but five hundred thousand showed up.[3] Across the world, sister marches brought the number of protestors to 5 million.[4] As the sun began to set, my friend passed me his flask of whiskey and I took another sip. I rubbed my hands together to try to keep them warm. But eventually, the whiskey wore off and my fingers grew numb again. I was exhausted and cold. It was time to head home.

Back at my friend's apartment, we turned on the TV. I was expecting the historical moment I had just experienced to be reflected on the news. Instead, there was Sean Spicer, in his first appearance as press secretary, delivering the kind of chastisement you'd expect from a sitcom dad venting rage at his family after returning home from a shit job. For minutes, Spicer went on a bizarre tirade, attacking the press for allegedly lying about the size of the crowds at Trump's inauguration the day before, and detailing why they may have appeared smaller and less enthusiastic. ("This was the first time in our nation's history that floor coverings have been used to protect the grass on the Mall!")[5]

I sat stupefied as Spicer went on and on about the same place in Washington that, when I'd left it moments before, had still been crowded with throngs of protesters. And yet he made zero mention of the Women's March. Instead, it was all about the inauguration. He insisted that it was "the largest audience to ever witness an inauguration—period—both in person and around the globe." Which was, of course, patently false. But there it was, delivered directly to the American people because the major news networks were covering it live—unprepared, in the moment, to forcefully contradict the lie of it.

The narrative of the day, despite the largest protest ever seen in a single day in the United States, was the debate over the size of the crowd who had watched Donald Trump's presidential inauguration.

I watched slack-jawed from my friend's couch as Spicer wrapped his bizarre speech, and members of the press lobbed questions at his back as he swiftly exited the briefing. In that moment, I realized we were up against something formidable: where we turn our attention constructs the fabric of our reality. Here, Trump's administration was setting a clear standard: *We will talk about what we want to talk about, and nothing else.* They had declared a war on our collective reality. All they had to do was to simply say *nothing*.

This wasn't entirely new, of course. Going silent or redirecting our attention in the face of unpleasant facts or an inconvenient reality has become a time-honored tradition in politics: I remember George W. Bush's White House press secretary Scott McClellan denying knowledge of the reports that we were sending terrorism suspects to black sites to be tortured—even when that information was front-page news. ("You've never heard of any allegations like that?" "That's a new one."[6]) Then there was the blanket media ban—lifted once Obama took office—that forbade journalists from taking any photos of the ceremonies at Dover Air Force Base marking the arrival of the caskets of fallen soldiers. There's no easier way to deny the reality of the costs of war than to rob Americans of the ability to collectively *see* those costs.

But more disheartening than Spicer and the Trump administration ignoring the marches by pushing a false and distracting narrative was seeing how those on the Left—and so many in the media—discounted the marches as well. I had followed the challenges that marked the birth of the Women's March. The original organizers, who were white, initially billed it as the "Million Woman March," which understandably struck many as tone-deaf and co-optive since the "Million Man March" was organized and undertaken by black men. To the original organizers' credit, they renamed the event and welcomed veteran organizers of color on board—Linda Sarsour, Tamika Mallory, and Carmen Perez.

Still, there were other bumps along the way: the confusion over whether the focus of the protest should be on Trump's election, or on more specific issues like women's rights and immigrant rights. Then there was the conflict that emerged when some white women voiced their discomfort in response to the conversations about privilege that was burgeoning online—arguing that it was divisive and that we should come together as *women*, no matter our race, sexual orientation, or gender identity. All of this was on full display since the protest, from its very beginnings, was organized online—starting with Facebook. Yet the organizers delivered, making it possible for half a million of us to gather in Washington, D.C.—and millions more to follow suit around the world.

The challenges and confusion that unfolded in the days leading up to the protest were covered by many news outlets and often used as fodder for justifying the conceit that protest doesn't accomplish anything. A sampling of headlines from the immediate lead-up to and aftermath of the protests in Washington: "When Protest Fails,"[7] "Why the Women's March on Washington Has Already Failed,"[8] "How the Women's March Failed Women."[9]

This all dovetailed quite nicely with statements from Trump's "counselor to the President," Kellyanne Conway, who went on ABC News to tell Americans she "didn't see the point" of the protests.[10] She also relished directing our attention to who *wasn't* in attendance: former president Barack Obama and Hillary Clinton.

Which was true. They weren't there.

The lack of political figureheads was notable—leading many to ask whom we might turn to for guidance and leadership in the vacuum that opened up after the election, when both Obama and Clinton delivered conciliatory messages to the American people: that we must peacefully accept Trump, that we must give him a fair chance.

Yet a huge number of Americans refused to do this, and made that known by marching in the streets. Some called it pointless. Others called it democracy in action.

I want to understand the distance between those two beliefs.

PROTEST DOESN'T WORK
(EXCEPT WHEN IT DOES)

MMEDIATELY FOLLOWING THE ELECTION, AMERICANS were faced with a new reality—a new "normal" in which checks and balances are obliterated and executive orders pushed through at a frantic pace. It's easy to feel inundated by the news of the day. Our sense of time has altered such that it's become a predictable refrain that we can't believe it's only been one month, six months, one year, since Trump moved into the White House. Alongside the daily assaults on our sensibilities—or our lives and livelihoods outright—are an increasing number of opportunities to take action: by calling representatives, signing petitions, marching in the streets, visiting our local representatives' offices. But if we don't believe these actions will have any impact, we're less inclined to take part in them.

There's a fascinating dissonance between how we view political action and protest today and in the past. We're all familiar with the monumental shifts that came about as a result of protest in the civil rights era. It's become a cultural touchstone, an integral part of our public school curriculum.

When we recall the civil rights movement, we tend to discuss it with a general reverence for the leaders and protesters who participated. But at the time, the majority of Americans did not support actions that were at the heart of it. A full 61 percent of Americans disapproved of Freedom Riders—the folks who rode interstate buses in the South, challenging the segregation that was still going strong despite its unconstitutionality. Fifty-seven percent of Americans at the time thought that black Americans were *hurting* their chances of being integrated in the South by taking part in these kinds of protests and demonstrations.[11] In other words, they didn't feel that protesters were being *pragmatic*.

The same shift in the perception of protests occurred around the Vietnam War. At the time the war was raging, 71 percent of Americans disapproved of protests against it. By the 1980s, that number had dropped to roughly 50 percent.[12]

It's a stiff shot of context, one that might be useful to down before we turn our eye to contemporary protest movements. Recognizing our tendency toward *inaction* and our likelihood to change our minds about political and social justice movements after the fact can be hugely instructive for our present moment. Today, the majority of Americans—68 percent—have either negative or neutral views of the Black Lives Matter movement.[13] It's consistent with what we see throughout history: Americans don't have a particularly high opinion of protests or protesters. Except when they end up turning the tide of history. Then, we call them necessary, instructive, even inevitable.

Part of that dissonance comes down to the language and stories we use to talk about political action in the past. So much is in the way it's told. Rosa Parks, for example, is often written as a stereotypically grandmotherly figure—a woman who was simply tired when she refused to get up from her seat. To speak of her this way is not only to get it wrong, but to strip her of the intentionality and politics that drove her. As one historical account of the civil rights era for children puts it:

> One day on her way home from work Rosa [Parks] was tired and sat down in the front of the bus. As the bus got crowded she was asked to give up her seat to a European American man, and she refused. The bus driver told her she had to go to the back of the bus, and she still refused to move. It was a hot day, and she was tired and angry, and became very stubborn.*

We rely on these received narratives of history—usually short, anecdotal—to give us a cohesive sense of what happened and why, cause and effect. Too often, these anecdotes convey the notion that moments of political change were unplanned, fateful, driven by some invisible hand of social justice. Stripped of nuance—and often of the "failures" before the successes—history assumes the uncomplicated inevitability of gravity.

---

* Jonathan Birnbaum, Clarence Taylor, eds. *Civil Rights Since 1787: A Reader on the Black Struggle* (New York: New York University Press, 2000), 446.

But, of course, the reality is always more complex.

"People always say that I didn't give up my seat because I was tired," Parks has said, "but that isn't true. I was not tired physically, or no more tired than I usually was at the end of a working day. I was not old, although some people have an image of me as being old then. I was forty-two. No, the only tired I was, was tired of giving in."[14] Young, able-bodied, and clear about what she was doing, Parks did not have a sense of certainty about the outcome of her actions, but she was certain of her political convictions: "I would like to be known as a person who is concerned about freedom and equality and justice and prosperity for all people."[15]

Without sufficient context, we're often led to believe that Parks's action was spontaneous and organic, despite the fact that it was deliberately choreographed: Parks had been the secretary of the Montgomery NAACP office for twelve years by the time she refused to give up her seat on that bus. Nine months before Parks's action, fifteen-year-old Claudette Colvin had been arrested for doing the very same. When E. D. Nixon, the president of the Montgomery NAACP, and others began discussing a bus boycott, they decided that Parks would make a better face for the campaign as Colvin was deemed too young, feisty, and dark-skinned to leverage the sympathies of white people. [16] As Colvin recalls: "My mother told me to be quiet about what I did . . . She told me: 'Let Rosa be the one. White people aren't going to bother Rosa—her skin is lighter than yours and they like her.'"[17]

Parks was not simply a sweet old lady who was tired. She—and her allies—were tired of a very particular kind of bullshit and set about planning an action that might have the highest likelihood of changing the tide of history.

Our anemic historical narratives usually edit out agency and intentionality. They also tend to miss another critical aspect of movements: the less stirring stories of the build-up before the successes, the quieter groundwork that was laid, the earlier "failures" that all led eventually—but usually not before many years had passed—to victory.

Before Rosa Parks, there wasn't just Colvin. There were thousands of other black men and women who sat in "whites only" sections of buses or trains, refusing to move. It was their work that paved the way, making it impossible for Americans to ignore what was becoming an increasingly persistent movement.

And that *is* often how it happens—a relatively small group of committed folks continue to force the question even when many, perhaps the majority, of Americans disagree or would prefer to not have to reckon with it. History books typically opt for the compelling photos that show thousands of people gathered in protest, giving us the sense that real change only comes when massive groups of people take action together. But the reality is that smaller groups committed to taking action over time have had some of the greatest impact.

Take the protest group ACT UP: In the 1980s, people who became sick with HIV/AIDS were widely reviled. The illness was referred to as "gay cancer" or the "gay plague." Sufferers were socially shunned, the bodies of those who died collected by city health-care workers and stuffed in plastic garbage bags. some of ACT UP's most notable actions had only somewhere between seven and fifteen hundred people participating, but they were dogged in their commitment to change. That movement pushed for new HIV/AIDS drugs that helped save millions of lives—and destigmatized the illness, as well as homosexuality more generally, in the process. [18]

We see the same kind of success from small and dedicated groups of organizers today. In the aftermath of the Sandy Hook Elementary School shooting, activist Eric Liu helped organize folks in Washington State. Their local Alliance for Gun Responsibility became a model for other states after they successfully organized and won statewide ballot initiatives, including one that implemented universal background checks.[19] When we surface these narratives about the reality of what it takes to make change possible, it's easier to recognize how *not inevitable* these historical sea changes are. If we see some of the challenges and "failures" that movements have faced in history, we develop a much clearer sense of how necessary they are to subsequent successes.

Perhaps this oversight reflects our American aversion to anything that speaks of "failure." But to erase movement "failures" is to erase the work—of showing up time and again with the understanding that it will take more than a single protest or action to lead to change, the understanding that this doesn't make the action any less vital to our eventual success.

This oversight relates, too, to our narrow American definition of "success." The American Dream is rooted in the conceit that we are always moving on up, obtaining better lives—usually as defined by the accumulation of more belongings. It's a narrative that doesn't allow much space for imaginings of different visions of success: sustainability, equality, justice. And because the narrative is so ingrained, it can make us blind to the realities that don't tidily fit within it: 90 percent of Americans born in the 1940s were financially better off than their parents. But only 50 percent of Americans born in the 1980s will do better than their parents, despite the fact that they're better educated.[20]

All of these tendencies in the way historical narratives are shaped—in textbooks and the popular consciousness—give us a skewed sense not only of how political change happens but of our rightful role in it. It's a little like trying to learn about sex by watching porn: anyone looking to it as a primer or how-to is bound to be sorely disappointed (and likely disappointing) when they try to replicate what they've seen.

WHEN WE SEE HISTORY as a timeline composed of only the most pivotal moments, we project a narrative of intuitive cause and effect. Hard-fought battles for equality and social change take on the aura of inevitability, of pragmatism, common sense. But what we deem to be pragmatic or common sense is constantly changing, subject to the whims of our current sociopolitical moment. Which means there can be no conversation about "common sense" without examining how it hinges on privilege.

The fact that the majority of Americans thought black Americans during the civil rights era were *hurting* the integration cause by protesting speaks volumes. To believe that nonviolent protest is unnecessary, pointless, over-the-top, or reflective of an unreasonable "impatience" presupposes that your day-to-day existence is tolerable and acceptable. In the heyday of the civil rights movement, a constant criticism leveled at activists and leaders was that they were being too impatient, that change would come in time through the passage of laws and the court system enforcing those laws. In his famous letter, written while in a Birmingham jail, Martin Luther King, Jr., responded by saying,

> We have waited for more than three hundred and forty
> years for our God-given and constitutional rights . . . I
> guess it is easy for those who have never felt the stinging
> darts of segregation to say "wait." But when you have
> seen vicious mobs lynch your mothers and fathers at will
> and drown your sisters and brothers at whim; when you
> have seen hate-filled policemen curse, kick, brutalize, and
> even kill your black brothers and sisters with impunity;
> when you see the vast majority of your twenty million
> Negro brothers smothering in an airtight cage of poverty
> in the midst of an affluent society . . . when you are

harried by day and haunted by night by the fact that
you are a Negro, living constantly at tiptoe stance, never
quite knowing what to expect next, and plagued with
inner fears and outer resentments; when you are forever
fighting a degenerating sense of "nobodyness"—then you
will understand why we find it difficult to wait.[21]

In other words, "wait" is what you say when waiting does not
threaten your, or your family's, daily existence and dignity.

TODAY, WE SHARE A fairly common understanding of the necessity of the civil rights movement. We respect the quiet dignity
of protesters in black-and-white photographs that depict them
sitting at lunch counters while crowds of white people taunted
them, pouring sugar and ketchup over their heads. I think of
these protests—and the way they were denigrated or discounted
by so many Americans at the time—whenever I read yet another
think piece by a journalist or pundit presuming the ineffectuality
of protest today. When I get into conversations with folks at bars
who shrug and say, *What's the point?* True, a single protest like the
Women's March will not suddenly change the course of history,
but then, would we ever say that lunch-counter sit-ins were a failure because they did not immediately overturn Jim Crow laws?

This dissonance between how we view the role of Americans
in creating history in the past versus the present signals our need
to expand our definitions of pragmatism, failure, and success
when it comes to political action and engagement.

Part of this work is recognizing that different types of protest
and political action have different goals. There are two general categories of direct action: expressive and instrumental. The latter is

tied to a specific external outcome—to oust someone from office or to have a specific demand met. Expressive actions are more concerned with affirming and building solidarity.[22] Substantive social or political change relies on both types of action. The problem is that we tend to only attach value to instrumental actions.

Expressive actions get short shrift, yet they're vital to building and offering people a vision of an alternative world, and fostering a sense of joy and solidarity among those protesting. They're integral to forging community and laying the groundwork for more actions—including instrumental actions. In short, expressive actions help build the infrastructure for the reality that we are insisting upon.

Demonstrations like the lunch counter sit-ins combined both of these elements to achieve something else: a prefigurative intervention. As writer and activist Andrew Boyd puts it, "The students' actions—mixed-race groups of people violating the law by sitting at lunch counters and demanding to be served—foreshadowed victory and prefigured the world they wanted to live in: they were enacting the integration they wanted."[23] They were demonstrating what a necessary future looked like for those whose imaginative powers might have failed them. It's an important reminder of the strength in seizing and modeling power rather than politely waiting for it to be offered to us.

With such a fractured media landscape, direct action like this also enables us to do something increasingly vital: forcibly grasp control of moments of collective reality, creating a powerful *now* in which we are actors in, rather than passive consumers of, history.

SUCCESSFUL FAILURES

MARTIN LUTHER KING, JR.'S "I Have a Dream" speech is widely hailed as one of the greatest speeches in history. He delivered it in 1963 to a quarter of a million Americans during the March on Washington. Three years later, polls showed that only 33 percent of Americans had positive feelings about King. In fact, the speech was not lauded—or even widely discussed—until after his death in 1968.[24]

The way we talk about history has collapsed the reality of this timeline, as well as the intentionality behind King's speech. King was an incredibly powerful speaker, and it's true that parts of the "I Have a Dream" speech were improvised—something often emphasized in textbooks and articles. Less is made of the fact that King had delivered key parts of the speech twice before to crowds in North Carolina and Detroit.[25] It was meticulously crafted and practiced in front of different audiences; the details surrounding his delivery were similarly choreographed: a high-quality sound system, the staging of the Lincoln Memorial in the background, the press gathered in a place to get a full view of King.

Despite all of that effort, his powerful speech did not immediately lead to a concrete instrumental outcome. King wanted those in power to pay attention to the movement, to address the concerns of black Americans, but his focus was on speaking to Americans directly: "I say to you today, my friends, so even though we face the difficulties of today and tomorrow, I still have a dream."[26] It's an important reminder that, though presidents and politicians cycle in and out of power, there is a permanent locus of power, one that King and all effective social justice movement leaders recognize: us.

THE WOMEN'S MARCH ON Washington wasn't the only action organized by women in the wake of an election upset: in November 1980, roughly 1,500 women converged on the Pentagon, protesting sexism, militarism, and nuclear proliferation. The Women's Pentagon Action occurred just two weeks after Ronald Reagan was elected as president. Yet nowhere in their statement or action did they even mention Reagan. In her book *Direct Action: Protest and the Reinvention of American Radicalism*, L.A. Kauffman writes that they treated the election "almost like a non-event." This was deliberate, as one of the organizers, Ynestra King, pointed out:

"There was a whole discussion with the organization about who are we doing this for . . . And basically we really believed that we were doing it for ourselves."[27]

Speaking to *each other* and building solidarity is a vital role of protest and direct action. It's an important reminder in a post-Trump era marked by ongoing exhortations to "reach across the aisle." While I cannot argue against the importance of having conversations with those whose views are different from our own, I *do* want to emphasize the importance of connecting and bolstering solidarity with those who share our core values. Sure, we don't want to get caught up in preaching to the choir, but we don't want to overcorrect to the point that we forget about the existence of the choir—that powerful body that only thrives as long as, and in as much as, we regularly sing our songs together.

There's also something to be said for the magnetism of the choir—being passionate and joyfully united, whether in song or some other action of solidarity, often serves as an invitation, bringing others into the fold.

Activism during the era of internet primacy offers up more opportunities and pitfalls on this front. There is, of course, the "echo chamber" effect, whereby social media algorithms and filters can function as blinders, making it harder for us to identify where our voices fit within a broader conversation. But there are other kinds of profoundly effective echoing that occur online: the #metoo hashtag went viral in October 2017, sparking a movement that drew the participation of women from across the country, all of whom testified to their personal experiences of sexual assault and harassment.

What started as a handful of actresses in Hollywood speaking out became a forceful movement joined by women from a wide array of backgrounds. Just weeks after the allegations against movie producer Harvey Weinstein began to gain steam, seven hundred thousand Latina farmworkers published an open letter, pledging their solidarity and making clear that it was a problem they, too, had been fighting and would continue to fight alongside them:

> We work in the shadows of society in isolated fields and packinghouses that are out of sight and out of mind for most people in this country. Your job feeds souls, fills hearts and spreads joy. Our job nourishes the nation with the fruits, vegetables and other crops that we plant, pick and pack.
>
> Even though we work in very different environments, we share a common experience of being preyed upon by individuals who have the power to hire, fire, blacklist and otherwise threaten our economic, physical and emotional security . . .
>
> In these moments of despair, and as you cope with scrutiny and criticism because you have bravely chosen to speak out against the harrowing acts that were committed against you, please know that you're not alone. We believe and stand with you.[28]

#Metoo created a powerful echo—a chorus of voices that laid bare a social epidemic and helped foster an environment ripe for the implementation of lasting and enforceable change.

Much ink has been spilled over whether the internet is a revolutionary platform for organizing, or a palliative—offering up smaller actions like signing petitions that too often fail to scale up to movements that promise broader impact and change. It is, of course, both of these things. It offers unprecedented opportunities for communication and organizing, but it's most effective when it's used as a tool in conjunction with face-to-face organizing and action. There's a reason Occupy Wall Street garnered so much attention as a movement, and it wasn't just because of their effective online framing and messaging. It was because there were thousands of people in cities across the country—and around the world—marching in the streets, camping out in public, and otherwise doing the unexpected: *becoming visible* and *taking up space* as political beings. Seeing and recognizing each other. Communing and seeking solidarity in a society that often encourages us to cordon off our needs and hopes as private affairs.

These are not the kinds of movement achievements or successes that are commonly acknowledged by the press. As in the case of the Women's March in 2017, the press largely shrugged in response to the Women's Pentagon Action. *The Washington Post* called it a "60s-style protest" and quoted an unnamed navy official: "I guess they're having fun . . . I bet these chicks don't even know why they're here."[29] Meanwhile, for the women who participated, and for the broader peace movement, the protest was an important moment. In Kauffman's interviews with attendees and organizers, there was a common refrain: what they had seen was an unprecedented combination of strategies from different movements that had powerfully converged in the Women's Pentagon Action—civil disobedience from the civil rights and anti-nuclear movements, guerrilla theater from sixties feminists and Yuppies, collective process and decentralized organization from anarchists and feminists.[30] Yet this kind of momentum and synthesis went largely unrecognized by outsiders. From the vantage point of the wider public, it was a non-event, disparaged by the press.

Key solidarity work had occurred, but the only way for that narrative—and its momentum—to work was for those involved in the protests to *keep moving forward* despite the fact that few were paying attention. They didn't require Reagan to respond; hell, they didn't even utter the man's name during their protests. Many of the women involved in these protests returned the following year for a similar protest. And in subsequent years, women at the core of this movement went on to rally around the cause of nuclear disarmament—commanding the attention of millions around the world and ushering in an era of nuclear de-escalation.[31]

In the aftermath of the 2017 Women's March, there was a similar momentum and domino effect. Ten months after that day of historic protests, *The Huffington Post* published an article profiling multiple women who were inspired by the march to run for office. They not only ran, they won—unseating GOP men.[32] Organizers of the Women's March also helped push right-wing TV personality Bill O'Reilly off the air in April of 2017 (using the hashtag #DropOReilly) after it came to light that Fox News had paid more than $13 million in settlements to women who accused O'Reilly of workplace harassment.[33]

These stories of causality and momentum are often drowned out by the noise generated by headlines breathlessly calling our actions "failures"—often before we even carry them out. They're compelling historical narratives to remind ourselves of in the wake of actions like the Women's March on Washington and Trump's general disregard for it. Our momentum and power does not hinge on a handful of people acknowledging or fearing us, but on building and solidifying our movement.

When we resurface these stories from history, we gain the ability to see the power of protest and direct action. Without these vital narratives, we remain blind to protest's power—continuing to dismiss or discount movements that have the potential to—and *are*—making history. Right now.

What if we could recognize the value of political moments and movements *as they happen* rather than waiting for history books to ascribe them meaning?

ON OCTOBER 15, 2011, a crowd of some ten thousand Occupy Wall Street protesters and supporters marched to Times Square from Zuccotti Park in Lower Manhattan.[34] As the sun began to set, I stood on the outskirts of the crowd, penned in by barricades. Passers-by would occasionally stop and stare. A handful looked for gaps in the barricades and joined in; others walked by without paying us any mind. One man in particular marks my memory: wearing a suit, arms freighted with shopping bags from nearby stores, he paused to take it in, his mouth pursed in disgust. "Get a job," he spat. "I've got three," a man near me yelled back. It wasn't the first time I'd seen someone express outright animosity toward protesters, but it didn't stop me from being perplexed by the vehemence of that outrage.

Still, he was not emblematic of the general response to OWS. During the height of the protests, a large number of Americans (one poll put it at 59 percent)[35] supported the message of OWS that income inequality had reached grotesque levels. Unfortunately, that didn't necessarily translate into widespread support for the OWS movement itself. Unlike the more cohesive narratives we attach to the civil rights movement (with separate actions around the country over a number of years understood to be part of a unifed movement), protest movements since that era tend to be discussed as isolated events, disconnected from their broader legacies—both what intuitively came before, and what follows from them.

When the protestors were evicted from Zuccotti Park on

November 15, 2011, ending a nearly two-month occupation, pundits and journalists competed over who got to declare the pointlessness and failure of the movement.[36] Take journalist Wray Herbert's "Why 'Occupy Wall Street' Fizzled," published in *The Huffington Post*:

> Its message, beyond disdain for the rich, was never
> entirely clear to many Americans, and indeed its various
> protests fizzled without much to show—no new leaders,
> no legislative victories or political change of any kind. If
> anything, the national mood favored liberal ideas, yet the
> Occupy protestors never showed any kind of solidarity.
> The movement is now dead, and will be no more than a
> footnote to history.[37]

It's an example of how these tired—and inaccurate—narratives around the expectations and "inefficacy" of protest keep cropping up despite so much historical evidence to the contrary. And it's a clear example, in particular, of the failure to recognize the power in expressive actions. While OWS protesters were initially dismissed as a handful of college kids, the movement had grown rapidly, mobilizing participants across age, race, and class lines. Major labor unions like the AFL-CIO and SEIU endorsed the protests, with union members joining the ranks at marches and rallies. It was stirring to see older union organizers leading crowds in songs like "Roll the Union On"—younger protesters learning the lyrics for the first time. Part of the popularity of the OWS message had to do with timing: the 2008 recession had left millions of Americans without—or struggling to hold onto—their homes. Ninety percent of the financial gains that were made in the wake of the recession went to the wealthiest 1 percent of the people in this country[38]—a shocking statistic given that, between 2007 and 2010, the median net worth of families *went down* by 40 percent.[39]

OWS emerged out of this time, and was able to effectively capture the feelings of pain and outrage with a "We are the 99 percent" slogan that spread like wildfire. Americans posted photos of themselves with messages telling their personal stories of foreclosures and medical and student-loan debt that had left them bankrupt or struggling.

The visibility of so many Americans struggling allowed a sense of solidarity. Instead of thinking of their hardships as some aberration or personal shortcoming, they were situating themselves in a different narrative: as a part of a huge contingent of Americans who were suffering because of broader institutional failures. That combination of powerful individual storytelling with a more unified "99 percent" framework went viral—becoming one of the most broadly inclusive and sticky protest messages we've seen in history. Even after OWS had faded from headlines, the "1 percent" frame continues to surface in protests, headlines, and political rhetoric.

To call OWS a "footnote" to history or a "dead" movement reflects a historical ignorance and myopia. There are countless examples of its momentum and impact in the political sphere.

The movement dramatically impacted the 2012 election, forcing both Mitt Romney and Obama to address inequality and corporate greed. A key part of Obama's winning strategy was to tap into Americans' growing frustration—which OWS helped crystallize—with big banks.[40] The same was true of New York City in 2013, when Bill de Blasio piggybacked on the OWS message with his "tale of two cities" narrative that addressed inequality. It was a winning story: after twenty years of Republican leadership, New Yorkers elected Democrat de Blasio in a landslide victory, replacing the three-term billionaire Michael Bloomberg as mayor.[41]

Many news and analysis stories that sought to explain why OWS "failed" continued to be published long after OWS protesters were evicted from Zuccotti Park—Herbert's article on why OWS "fizzled" appeared in July 2013, nearly two years after the eviction. This suggests a question: If the movement had fizzled and failed, why was he—why were so many of us—still talking about it?

OWS was not only successful in designing expressive actions or in influencing politicians; there are numerous instrumental actions that came out of its organizing infrastructure. After the occupation of Zuccotti Park ended, the movement evolved into different initiatives. In the wake of Hurricane Sandy, which devastated parts of New York City, it was Occupy Sandy that provided vital support for those who needed it most. When federal relief failed to arrive in time, Occupy picked up the slack, bussing volunteers and supplies to areas such as the Rockaways that were hardest hit by the storm.[42]

There were other OWS initiatives that emerged, too: Strike Debt organized events where people across the country could pitch in small amounts of money that were then used to buy medical and student loan debt from debt collectors for pennies on the dollar. Then, they forgave the debts. To date, they've raised over $700,000, allowing them to purchase and forgive $32 million in debts.[43] In the process, they shed light on the broader inhumanity of a financial system that buys and sells the debt of millions of Americans to predatory collections agencies for a fraction of the original price. Another Occupy offshoot teamed up with local activists in cities across the country to take over vacant bank-owned homes to help homeless families reoccupy them.[44]

The people and infrastructure behind OWS also directly influenced the growth of a number of other political movements—from the Fight for $15 to raise the minimum wage, to the Black Lives Matter movement, to the rise of presidential contender Bernie Sanders, who, despite not receiving the Democratic nomination, remains one of the most influential politicians and movement leaders today.[45] Right now, parallel to a White House that has never more directly represented the 1 percent, we have a series of powerful grassroots movements that are fighting and advocating for the majority of Americans.

The Fight for $15 has successfully fought for raises for 22 million Americans and has grassroots campaigns in hundreds of cities.[46] Black Lives Matter chapters continue to organize actions that bring thousands of Americans together, forcing the nation to reckon with fundamental questions of justice and equality. Bernie Sanders continues to rally Americans around a push for single-payer health insurance that would cover everyone in his "Medicare for all" campaign—a cause that's gaining ground. Sixty percent of Americans now support guaranteed health care coverage for all.[47]

This type of ripple effect isn't unique to Occupy Wall Street; it's an inherent component of political movements.

WE TEND TO BE stingy about what we call a successful protest or action. Generally, unless it has a very clear, achievable demand that is met within a short period of time, it slips through the cracks of our popular consciousness until, perhaps, enough time has passed that it can join the ranks of the Cliff's Notes versions of history that crop up in our textbooks. But if we expand our parameters—and our timeline—of what a successful or strategic protest might look like, our political landscape becomes *much* more interesting. And our power as Americans to shape history becomes incontrovertible.

The lead-up to the 2016 presidential elections featured a prime example of how a "failed" movement had a powerful impact on our political reality. While Bernie Sanders did not receive the Democratic nomination, the popularity of his platform forced Hillary Clinton to the left. By the time Sanders conceded, Clinton was advocating for free college education and raising the minimum wage.[48]

Simply being a countervailing force or voice can alter the course of history, even if it's unlikely that your viewpoint or initiative will win wholesale.

In May 2011, the nonprofit environmental organization Our Children's Trust announced a lawsuit on behalf of American youth. A handful of teenagers are suing the federal government and all fifty states for policies that have contributed to climate change and violated their constitutional right to life, liberty, and property.[49] The US government and industries have tried to shut the landmark lawsuit down, but it keeps moving forward, winding its way through the system, gaining momentum and attention. It's already inspiring similar actions. After the deadly 2017 forest fires in central Portugal, a handful of Portuguese children decided to take action: they crowdfunded to raise money for the legal expenses to sue forty-seven European nations for failing to take action on climate change.[50]

It would make history if either of these lawsuits won, but in many ways the lawsuits are *already* winning: they've generated scores of news headlines and interviews with the young people who are the plaintiffs. The idea that a group of children can sue a country—or an entire continent—is revolutionary in its own right, igniting our imaginations, pushing against received notions of pragmatism, and expanding our perceptions of what's possible.

It shifts the conversation, modeling what it looks like to earnestly hold those in power to the expectations they should be meeting.

If this is naïveté, it's a kind of naïveté we need to cultivate.

ON JANUARY 21, 2017, millions of people participated in women's marches around the world. The action mobilized many who had never been to a protest before. In Washington D.C., I talked to three women in their sixties who had traveled from a small town in Colorado. None of them had ever attended a protest before, which I found fascinating since the civil rights movement and opposition to the Vietnam War were in full effect when they were in their teens and twenties. But here they were *now*.

When I asked why they had been moved to come out, one of the women said that as she inched closer to the end of her life, she couldn't stand the idea that the political situation was worse than it was when she was growing up. To see a professed sexual predator in the White House outraged her. Another woman told me about how folks in her neighborhood had recently banded together to help raise money to cover the hospital bills of some of their neighbors. It was so nice, she said, to have community to count on, but she was left with the feeling that "it shouldn't be like this. We shouldn't have to rely on our neighbors to cover our medical bills."

Whatever their personal reasons may be, many Americans feel our current political situation has become untenable. Enough to get them out of their homes, onto planes and trains, and into the streets.

But the question of how long this energy will last is an important one. And if we continue to hold onto these impossibly narrow and ahistorical notions of what "successful" protest or action looks like, we're inclined to lose our momentum quickly.

Just a week after the Women's March, Trump issued an executive order banning refugees and other travelers from seven Muslim-majority countries from coming to the United States. Americans immediately mobilized, holding protests and rallies at airports in cities across the country. Yet parallel to this remarkable turnout and energy was a piece of analysis that went viral in the days after these protests. "The Immigration Ban is a Head-fake, and We're Falling For It," written by Jake Fuentes, outlines what the author believed to be a strategy by the Trump administration to consolidate power by "distracting" us with an unconstitutional executive order.[51]

Fuentes argued "the 'resistance' is playing right into Trump's playbook." He also recommended that, if we really want to oppose this consolidation of power, we need to "stop believing that protests alone do much good . . . Protesters get all kinds of feel-good that they're among fellow believers and standing up for what's right, and they go home feeling like they've done their part."

Fuentes implied that by protesting a legitimately horrendous piece of legislation that barred thousands of refugees from a safe haven, we were falling into some sort of trap. The argument was a remarkable display of privilege: it's nearly impossible to imagine that Fuentes would make this argument if a family member were being held at an airport, facing forced return to a country where they risked arrest, or far worse, because of the whims of a bigoted president. Fuentes also cynically implied that those protesting were somehow incapable of paying attention to more than one issue. No one I know who protests goes home and pats themselves on the back as though they've done all that's required of them. To even know when and where a protest is happening, you have to be regularly following the news, usually participating in groups that are discussing recent events and news on a daily basis. In other words, you are constantly being made aware of how much more work needs to be done. About a dozen friends and colleagues sent me the article—offering it up as a narrative that might be useful, a way to understand the reality we were facing. Countless more people on Facebook posted the article alongside expressions of defeatism or concern: *Oh god. We're fucked.* Yet another cynical and misguided argument for the pointlessness of protest made the rounds.

Fuentes's piece was posted on *Medium*—an open platform where anyone can publish. It was clear why the piece was popular: It touched a nerve, speaking to our greatest fears that nothing we can do will change the outcome of our situation, that we are unknowing pawns in a diabolical political game. It was the perfect analysis for our defeatist selves, those parts of us that want nothing more than to pull the covers over our heads and pretend we have no power. At the bottom of Fuentes's piece was his bio: "Head of New Products @ Capital One." It was a dark poetry that progressives and folks on the Left were circulating cynical political analysis by someone who worked for the eighth-largest commercial bank in the country.

Fuentes and those who circulated his armchair analysis likely see themselves as pragmatists. But as history shows us, pragmatism does not exist in a vacuum. It's all too often a function of privilege. What one person deems pragmatic depends on what they believe to be possible, and what they believe to be *necessary.*

This is what happens when we accept the flawed narratives around protest and political engagement: We end up seeking out narratives that confirm what we're told, what we fear to be true. We cultivate a kind of fundamentalism—that we do not have power, that we cannot change anything, even though this flies in the face of history.

And while we worship at the altar of this defeatism, those in power can rest easy, knowing it's unlikely they'll be held accountable for their actions. Not when we've already convinced ourselves that we don't have the power to do so.

We end up advocating for our own powerlessness, defending the status quo while telling ourselves that we're being savvy, smart, pragmatic.

HOW WE GOT HERE

THE SUMMER LEADING UP TO the 2016 election, when Hillary vs. Bernie was still the question of the day, I went for a long walk with my friend J. The sun was starting to set, and there was an unseasonable chill in the air. She and I wandered the path on the outskirts of Prospect Park in Brooklyn, arms linked. "So, what do you think?" I asked her.

She paused, pursing her lips, her gait slowing. "I like Bernie's ideas," she told me, "but I don't think he'd get enough votes in the general election." That's why, she explained, she would be supporting Hillary Clinton. Keep in mind, this wasn't the general election, which was still on the horizon; it was the *primaries*. Yet she felt enough concern about his *future* popularity that she was putting her money on a different horse rather than casting a vote for Sanders to see whether other Americans might not be as interested in his ideas as she was.

I was surprised. Of the two of us, she had always struck me as the more optimistic and idealistic. This didn't seem to fit. But here we were, one of my closest friends and I, keeping each other warm and talking politics. When I pressed her on her logic, she said with finality: "I just don't think Bernie has what it takes to win."

That conversation plagued me then, and it plagues me now. I understood that she thought she was being pragmatic—supporting the "safer" candidate in the interests of avoiding an outcome in which someone whose principles seemed even further afield from hers might win. Meanwhile, I thought she was being cynical—refusing to put her weight behind her beliefs, which was making it *less* likely for them to be enacted. She and I both considered ourselves informed and engaged people. So how could our sense of involvement—of what it means to be an American who cares about the direction of this country—be so different?

Was J.'s perspective cynical or pragmatic? Was mine naive or pragmatic?

Of course, these questions have been around as long as politics has. There's always some balance between the world we want and the world we think is possible. Like our views on protest, these perspectives are deeply influenced by privilege, and by the common narratives we have around the political process.

HERE'S AN IMPORTANT NARRATIVE that's gone missing: Until 1990, 52 percent of Americans reported that the Democratic or Republican party represented their views. Since then, that number has dropped—reaching an all-time low of 39 percent in 2016.* Which means the majority of Americans going into the 2016 election *already* felt like neither party was speaking to their concerns. It's no wonder Trump and Sanders were drawing so much attention: they both seemed to represent a dramatic change from the norm—Sanders because of his unapologetically democratic socialist leanings, and Trump because of the image he sold as a self-made, self-funded, straight-shooter who would "drain the swamp" of Washington.

There's no doubt Hillary Clinton was the most qualified to be president, given her experience in and out of the White House. But that experience, and the way she framed it—knowing how to reach across the aisle, compromise, find ways to navigate a deeply problematic political system—is a tough thing to sell to people who have a growing sense that neither Democrats nor Republicans are addressing their needs to begin with. (Of course, Clinton was also a tough sell because we live in a society rife with misogyny, something I examine more closely in the next section of the book.) If the entire system is profoundly flawed, it's logical that Americans would want to elect someone who promises to overhaul it rather than someone whose most stirring message is that they know how to compromise and work within it.

Why would we be interested in reaching across the aisle if both sides of the aisle seemed like a bum deal? In 2017, roughly 40 percent of Americans chose to identify as Independent rather

---

* This makes some sense when we look at how those party platforms are consistently to the right of Americans' concerns or interests. Throughout earlier American history, organized labor and a more vibrant democratic socialist energy had a real impact on the political process—arguably helping to give us Roosevelt and the New Deal; Eisenhower's continuation of the GI Bill beyond wartime along with the interstate highway system; Nixon's Environmental Protection Agency (EPA) as well as Occupational Safety and Health Administration (OSHA). Over time, as those influences began to weaken, the rate of Americans opting not to vote rose.

than Democrat or Republican.[52] Right now, "dissatisfaction with government/poor leadership" is rated as the top problem in our country by Americans. And while I'm always skeptical of polls, it's worth noting that according to a recent one, 59 percent of Americans who are not registered to vote say they agree with the statement that they believe "nothing ever gets done" in government; 54 percent say "politics is so corrupt"; 42 percent say "there is no difference between Democrats and Republicans"; and 37 percent believe "it doesn't make much difference in my life."[53]

There's a risky leap in these statistics—from identifying a problematic reality ("politics is so corrupt") to *accepting* that reality ("it doesn't make much difference in my life"). Identifying a problem is vital to addressing it, but there's often a cynical conflation when it comes to politics: we identify what's wrong but skip over asking questions about how we might—how we must—change it. Instead, we assume it's unchangeable, limiting the space in which we feel we can operate, narrowing the scope of the problems we believe can and should be addressed.

This is what worried me after the conversation I had with my friend J. It's easy for cynicism to look like pragmatism when we accept received notions about what is and isn't reasonable to expect from politicians; it creates a race to the bottom in terms of what we're willing to tolerate. This policing of our expectations ends up functioning as a kind of self-censorship as we lower the bar, preemptively compromising the vision of the world we want to live in for the sake of being "reasonable." When we are "pragmatic" in this way, we offer up a compromise before even making a demand.

It's in this environment—in the vast gulf between the narratives we've been offered and the political desires we have—that Trump rose to power.

As shocking as the outcome of this election was for so many of us, it's difficult to argue it was *surprising*. One of the challenging truths we have to metabolize is that we have allowed our political system—and the way we talk about it—to erode to the point that someone like Trump could bubble to the top. The real risk now is in treating Trump as an aberration, not recognizing the broader structural problems that led to his election. We may get rid of Trump, but if we don't address the forces that led to his rise, it's only matter of time before it all happens again.

WHO'S IN CHARGE?

HOW COULD WE GET IT *so wrong?* There's no doubt most journalists dropped the ball in the lead-up to the 2016 presidential election. While it's clear that the majority of Americans—regardless of where we fall on the political spectrum—are dissatisfied with our political system, most media outlets continue to cover politics in the same horse-race fashion, parsing the differences between Democratic and Republican candidates, as though this is a sufficient encapsulation of our concerns.

But if a substantial number of Americans identify as Independents, and if so many Americans are dissatisfied with our current political situation, the media's focus is profoundly misplaced. Instead of the top-down approach of following the candidates at every campaign stop, there should be a shift to a bottom-up method, where reporters invest more time in speaking directly to Americans about their concerns at town halls, rallies, and other local gatherings—and then weighing those against what political candidates are or aren't addressing.

In the absence of a narrative that addresses our concerns and questions, elections—and politics more generally—remain disconnected from our daily lives. Our own day-to-day concerns— struggling to buy groceries or pay our rent because our paychecks aren't covering the cost of living, being sexually harassed or overlooked for promotion at work, reconfiguring our budgets to factor in having to pay for birth control out of pocket because our health insurance refuses to cover it—are hugely political. If we're led to believe that the political realm isn't a legitimate place where we can seek relief and remedy for these concerns, politics remains an abstract game—one in which we understand our primary roles to be spectators placing their bets on the outcome rather than actors who have the power to directly impact that outcome.

Too often, we're encouraged to think of the act of choosing between options—saying "yes" or "no"—as the bedrock of our democratic power. There's very little way to express "none of the above" or "this instead."

With a two-party system whose platforms have grown increasingly divergent from Americans' interests, our political "choice" has been reduced to a simple up or down vote on candidates who aren't addressing our wants and needs. Yet because the narratives we're continually offered seem to imply that this *should be enough,* it becomes easy for political engagement to look like a passive, once-every-four-years "yes" or "no" vote.

In this context, protests like Occupy Wall Street or the Women's March—even with, or *because* of their disorganization and surfeit of messages and demands—serve as the ultimate rejection of this "yes or no" mentality. They are the opposite of complacency and passivity. They are inconvenient and messy. And that's part of their power, particularly when those we've historically relied on to navigate the state and health of our democracy or represent us— politicians, pundits, and journalists—are asleep at the switch.

IN 1981, *New Yorker* writer George W. S. Trow published a strange little book called *Within the Context of No Context*. Written at a time when cable television was just starting to take off— expanding the programming offered to us beyond the three major networks of CBS, NBC, and ABC—Trow was concerned with how *we* might be changing along with our media diet. Referencing one of the more popular game shows at the time, Trow writes:

> The important moment in the history of television was the moment when a man named Richard Dawson, "host" of a program called *Family Feud*, asked contestants to guess what a poll of a hundred people had guessed would be the height of the average American woman. Guess what they've guessed. Guess what they've guessed the *average* is.[54]

More than thirty-five years before the concepts of "truthiness" and "alternate facts" were born, here was an earlier ancestor. In *Family Feud*, the goal of the show is not to arrive at the actual fact; it's to arrive at what we think most people think the fact is. Here, the value of the *actual fact* is discarded, and the opinion *becomes* the fact: it's the focus of conversation, the information we need to know in order to play the game and win.

It's another way of describing how the media tends to cover elections. Endless polls are run (often funded by news outlets hungry for sexy headlines), and networks provide around-the-clock coverage less focused on where the candidates stand on the issues than whether such a stance will hurt their chances of being elected.

Tune into any major news network after a presidential debate, and you'll be treated to a panel of news anchors and other highly coiffed talking heads, weighing in to tell us who "won"—the gold standard of which seems to be who gave the most compelling performance. This, of course, is the shit in which a reality-TV-show star like Donald Trump gets to be the pig. The notion that these talking heads should instead be digging into discussion about the potential impact each candidate might have on everyday Americans' lives if elected—our job security, wages, access to health care, chances of seeing an improvement in our general well-being—has come to seem quaint and naive. We keep inching (sprinting, really) further in this direction. During the 2008 election year, the major nightly news networks (ABC, NBC, and CBS) spent a cumulative 220 minutes on issues coverage; in 2016, we got a total of 32 minutes. That's the three networks combined over the full course of the election year—*32 minutes.*[55]

Meanwhile, the polls that are used to measure electability can often look like some version of *Family Feud.* When Barack Obama's admission that he'd tried cocaine before getting into politics hit the news back in 2007, the pollsters got cracking. A Scripps Howard survey asked Americans whether American voters were ready to accept a president who had tried cocaine as an adult. Fifty-eight percent of Americans said American voters were not ready.[56] *The New York Times* got in on the action, asking Americans whether most people they knew would vote for a presidential candidate who has ever used cocaine. Seventy-four percent said they would not.[57] But how different would these responses look if Americans were instead asked, "Are *you* ready to accept a president . . ." and "Would *you* vote for . . ."?

It's become so common to abstract the question—to think of ourselves as separate from "other Americans" or "people you know"—that it's not difficult to imagine people who consider themselves politically engaged making it through an entire election cycle without earnestly engaging with questions like: *Who do I think would really make a better candidate? What kind of vision or promises must a candidate offer me in order to earn my vote? What kind of person do I want to see in the White House? What does the America I want to see look like?*

In this flurry of vacuousness and circularity, there is no center: our political candidates launder their narratives to appeal to what they think is appealing to Americans; Americans launder their narratives to support the candidate that seems most appealing to other Americans; and the majority of media outlets discuss which candidate is deemed most appealing based on the polls they fund asking Americans which candidate they believe other Americans will find most appealing.

In other words, as Gertrude Stein put it: "There is no there there."

Or, as *The New York Times* reported the day of the 2016 presidential election: "Hillary Clinton has an 85% chance to win."[58]

FOR TROW, IT WAS *Family Feud.* For me, it was a 2007 episode of *Live with Regis and Kelly.* I was stuck in the waiting room of my dentist's office and had already read through the office copy of *Highlights* magazine. I turned my attention to the television. It was December, approaching the holiday season. A small American flag front and center, green and red coffee mugs and Christmas decorations punctuating the table, Regis Philbin tells Kelly Ripa about a recent holiday party he attended. He explains that he was seated next to the progressive broadcast journalist Amy Goodman at an event:

> **REGIS PHILBIN:** She says, "Well, I have a show on PBS, we cover global events."
> **KELLY RIPA:** Oh my gosh.
> **RP:** Global news . . . Well, excuse me, but what am I going to have in common with someone who covers global news?
> **KR:** What is the global news?

The audience laughs throughout as the exchange continues:

> **RP:** You may be better known than anybody else because they see you every day on television, but what have we got to say? Nothing.
> **KR:** Nothing. Nothing. And they already know what you've got going on because you've talked about it that day.
> **RP:** We've got nothing.
> **KR:** Right.
> **RP:** She asks, "So what do you do?" I say, "We talk about nothing."

KR: And then it's sweet though because like heady people who are very accomplished, they're very good at, like, you know, sounding interested. Like, "It must be fascinating what you do." And I'm like, *[Ripa adopts childish voice]* "It's very fun. We had hot toys on yesterday. And then today we're going to make our own shirts out of waste."

RP: You're absolutely right. You realize then . . .

KR: . . . your lack of contribution.

RP: What you're doing. You're doing . . .

RP & KR: *[in unison]* . . . nothing.

KR: Nothing. Gosh, how can you stand us?

RP: It's just so sad. It really is.[59]

There's an undercurrent of humor that slowly unravels until the spool comes to a stop the moment Ripa stares out at the audience, her voice shifting and becoming more plaintive as she demands of them—and us—"how can you stand us?" Then Philbin looks right at the camera, breaking the fourth wall with a voice saturated in judgment and disappointment. "It's just so sad. It really is."

Despite the fact that they host the show, they talk as if their show's content follows a similar inevitability as planets do their orbits. Their vapidity becomes an in-joke, but then it turns on the audience. You can sense authentic resentment and self-loathing bubbling to the surface, and when it does, they direct it at us.

But it's *daytime television*, you protest. *What do you expect?* Only, this tendency echoes far beyond daytime television.

Recall Charles Gibson and George Stephanopoulos, who were both criticized for the choice of questions they posed during the 2008 Democratic presidential debate—few of which addressed substantive policy issues. Among other things, Obama was questioned about his patriotism because he did not wear an American flag lapel pin. He was also questioned about remarks made by his former pastor Reverend Jeremiah Wright—remarks that Obama had already publicly repudiated a number of times. Gibson's justification for asking these questions? "It keeps coming up, again and again."[60] As though he were blind to the fact that the reason it kept coming up "again and again" was because people like him kept bringing it up.

Gibson and Stephanopoulos continually defended themselves by saying that the questions they asked were the questions *Americans* wanted answers to. On NPR's *Day to Day* show, Madeleine Brand asked senior national correspondent for ABC News Jake Tapper how he responded to criticism that the questions asked during the debate weren't of substance. Unprompted, he immediately brought up lapel pins:

> **JAKE TAPPER:** That was a question from a voter, the one about the flag pin.
> **MADELEINE BRAND:** Well, a voter who was chosen by ABC News.
> **JT:** Let me make it clear: There are differences; issues should be discussed. I can tell you from having been to Pennsylvania in the last week a number of times, all of them are issues that the voters care about. They care about the economy, they care about health care, they care about Iraq. They also care about who these people are . . . Many voters, especially swing voters, do have concerns about what are Barack Obama and Hillary Clinton's attitudes towards small-town working people, and Reverend Wright does interest them. Does the media in general focus too much on trivial stories like Reverend Wright, like the flag lapel pin? I'm not going to disagree with that notion.

MB: Well, either they're trivial or they're not.

JT: I'm putting trivial in air quotes. You can't see me doing it.

MB: But that gets to the heart of it. Are they trivial or are they legitimate questions about character? I think that what you're saying is the latter.

JT: I think that some of these stories are stupid and I think some of them say something about who people are.[61]

When pressed to answer for the vapidity of the questions, Tapper defensively pointed the finger at Americans, despite the fact that the questions were *chosen* by ABC. He insisted that Stephanopoulos and Gibson were merely reflecting Americans' concerns. Interestingly, he said it's "the media" that focuses too much on trivial stories—as though he weren't "the media" himself. We saw Tapper claiming to be above the prejudice and rumor that drives questions about Reverend Wright and Obama's patriotism. Yet, Tapper and his brethren make a living off generating and propagating the very rumor and prejudice that he claims to be above, even going so far as pointing the finger at "small-town working people."

Between Gibson's "It keeps coming up, again and again" and Tapper's refusal to identify himself as the media, we start to see how political conversations become so anemic, with those who have the power to shape conversations peddling in and fueling prejudices they claim not to hold.

Since the rise of Trump, Tapper seems to have stepped up and owned his role, going on the offensive and regularly taking Trump officials like Kellyanne Conway to task in live interviews. Yet there are others who have stepped in to fill Tapper's shoes.

In September 2016, two months before Americans headed to

the polls, daytime TV *Today* show co-host Matt Lauer was chosen to interview Trump and Clinton live on NBC. At one point during the conversation, Trump insists, "I was totally against the war in Iraq." It's a categorically false statement that Lauer completely ignores, simply moving on to his next question.[62] Tommy Vietor, a former aide to President Obama, posted on Twitter, "How in the hell does Lauer not fact-check Trump lying about Iraq? This is embarrassingly bad."[63] It was a perspective shared by many who watched the live conversations: the hashtag #laueringthebar started trending on social media. Throughout the thirty-minute interview, Trump talks over Lauer, a situation that flips when you see Lauer interviewing Clinton, interrupting her repeatedly and redirecting the conversation toward her use of a private email server when she was serving as secretary of state under Obama.

Roughly a third of the conversation is taken up with Clinton responding to allegations that she had jeopardized national security by using a private email server. By the time Lauer interviewed Clinton, the FBI had already released the report on their investigation into the issue. Just days before the televised conversation, *The Washington Post* published an article about that report, concluding that it contained "no major revelations." Yet Lauer continues to rehash the scandal, firing a volley of questions at Clinton, which she responds to by citing the findings of the report. At which point, Lauer takes a pre-chosen question from the audience: "Secretary Clinton, how can you expect those such as myself . . . to have any confidence in your leadership as president when you clearly corrupted our national security?" Americans who had tuned in to learn more about what Clinton's agenda as a potential president might be were instead treated to a bizarrely repetitive line of questioning—one that had already been exhausted by the twenty-four-hour news cycle.

IT'S MADDENING TO SEE the way the media reflexively points the finger back at Americans. As though the reason we aren't able to have substantive conversations and debate is because we're too idiotic to do anything but fixate on lapel pins, email servers, and other "scandals" that only remain scandals inasmuch as the media continues to perpetuate them.

Yet, Americans point right back—between the stereotypes of corrupt politicians and unethical journalists, it can feel like a general orgy of faithlessness. The problem is how neatly this dovetails with Donald Trump's direct attacks on politicians and the press. At a rally in Arizona, telling the crowd, "For the most part, honestly, these are really, really dishonest people. And they're bad people," or tweeting that journalists are the "enemy of the American people."[64]

We're all facing a failing political system and instead of fighting to hold people accountable and demanding change, we too often comfort ourselves by playing a game of hot potato—passing the responsibility for the degradation of our discourse back and forth. We're more comfortable adopting a cynical stance. We don't strive to hold each other accountable in a meaningful way, but instead compete to seem the least shocked at how low our expectations of each other—and the institutions that make a democracy thrive or die—have become.

ORIGINAL CYNIC

C YNICISM" HAS COME TO MEAN nearly the exact opposite of its original definition. "Cynic" comes from the fifth century B.C., when Diogenes the Cynic was kicking around Greece, purportedly living with hardly a possession to his name. He was a "parrhesiast" or "one who 'says all' despite the risk to himself."[65] It's a startling departure from what cynicism has come to mean today—an unreflective savviness, a posture that is about projecting how unfoolable you are. If those in power behave poorly, if corruption hits the headlines, the contemporary cynic shrugs and says, *I'm not surprised.* That posture cuts to the core of what we *expect* from others and from our democracy, which is why it's such an important indicator of the health of a democracy.

At its worst, cynicism informs a kind of universal skepticism, a phenomenon that media scholar Mark Andrejevic describes as, "the ostensibly democratic assertion that, thanks to generalized debunkery . . . any worldview is as defensible as any other."[66] This brand of cynicism elevates disbelief to a kind of blind faith that no faith can be had.

It has come to pervade our culture—evident in much of the media we encounter on a daily basis—so that when we point the finger at those in power for being responsible for our cynicism, they point right back.

In the vacuum of functional political coverage, the kind that holds those in power accountable and speaks to our concerns, political humor shows have come to fill the void.

The Colbert Report had only been on air for about six months when Stephen Colbert stepped into the spotlight, delivering a scathing satirical monologue at the White House Press Correspondents' Dinner on April 29, 2006, during George W. Bush's second term. I remember how uncomfortable it was to watch—many of Colbert's jokes were met with silence, and over the course of the speech, a handful of Bush aides and supporters walked out. When Colbert calls out the president for his utter contempt for facts, the camera pans to Bush's tight-lipped face, the effort to maintain a mask of bemused indifference painfully legible. Colbert cites the president's low approval ratings, encourages him to not be disheartened, and compares him to Rocky Balboa in *Rocky*—"the heart-warming movie of a man who is repeatedly punched in the face." In one of the more memorable moments, he mocks the president's staged responses to crises of the past five years:

> I stand by this man . . . because he stands for things. Not even for things, he stands *on* things. Things like aircraft carriers and rubble and recently flooded city squares. And that sends a strong message that no matter what happens to America, she will always rebound with the most powerfully staged photo ops in the world.

Colbert doesn't give the media a pass, either:

> Over the last five years, you people were so good—over tax cuts, WMD intelligence, the effect of global warming. We Americans didn't want to know, and you had the courtesy not to try to find out. Those were good times, as far as we knew. But, listen, let's review the rules. Here's how it works: the president makes decisions. He's the decider. The press secretary announces those decisions, and you people of the press type those decisions down. Make, announce, type. Just put 'em through a spell check and go home. Get to know your family again. Make love to your wife. Write that novel you got kicking around in your head. You know, the one about the intrepid Washington reporter with the courage to stand up to the administration. You know: fiction.[67]

While Colbert bombastically delivers the monologue in his right-wing talking-head character, it's clear that he's nervous. At one point, he flubs the set-up to a joke, pausing to start over. Millions of Americans would go on to watch his character grow more robust over the course of the nine-year run of *The Colbert Report*, but we can see it still taking form here, nerves and fear peeking through an affected bluster. Colbert later recalled that there were very few people laughing in the front row, and afterward "no one was even making eye contact with me . . . no one is talking to me in the whole damn room."[68]

It was the kind of discomfort and awkwardness that you might expect in the wake of someone breaking the social pact of nicety to speak truth to power. It was, in short, a moment of original cynicism in the vein of Diogenes.

A recording of Colbert's monologue soon shot to the top of the charts as the No. 1 album on iTunes.[69] His speech established a kind of collective, cathartic "now," a moment in which millions recognized their own outrage. Colbert's character was speaking to Americans in a way few others were.

The speech was effective because it clearly pointed to what the president and press *should* be doing. It was a reminder of the baseline for what we collectively knew we should be able to expect from people in positions of power: The president *should* provide substantive responses to crises and world events rather than staged photo ops. The press *should* be holding those in power accountable, questioning shoddy justifications for sending our nation to war.

Today, it's grown more challenging to locate a commonly shared baseline of ethics. With so much corruption, shamelessness, and incompetence occurring in plain sight, that baseline keeps shifting, leaving us with confusion around whether and when it's reasonable to feel outrage. It can be easier to simply throw up our hands and dig our heels into our lack of surprise.

The trope of the corrupt politician has become so widespread that the phrase is redundant. We don't often pause to parse it, or to think about the repercussions of perpetuating it. Academic

Steve Fielding recently pointed to the danger of this stereotype, as it "can only further reinforce mistrust in the public realm, a mistrust that some political forces seek to exploit." While many other commonly circulated stereotypes have grown less racist and sexist over the years, our political stereotypes have stayed much the same. Fielding writes, "The corrupt politician is one such stereotype, one that is neither racist nor sexist and seemingly acceptable to all . . . a convenient view, for it means we, the audience, the voters, are not to blame for anything: we are not to blame because we are the victims of a politics gone wrong."[70]

JUST AS WE'VE SEEN journalists fumble in response to the rise of political figures who seem immune to shame and scandal, so, too, have comedians. During Trump's presidential campaign, comedians had a field day, mocking his bombast. It was all too easy to not take him seriously. On *Saturday Night Live*, Alec Baldwin's orange-faced, anus-mouthed impersonation was born—with Baldwin delivering lines nearly identical to Trump's actual public remarks. Trump was treated as a ridiculous figure in much the same way that comedians treated figures like Sarah Palin when she ran as John McCain's vice presidential candidate in 2008. Tina Fey's Palin character became a mainstay on *Saturday Night Live*. Her physical affectations and lines brilliantly mirrored Palin, just like Baldwin's do Trump. Of, course, the main difference between Palin in 2008 and Trump in 2016 is that Palin didn't go on to win control of the White House.

Baldwin continues to play the buffoonish Trump character, but to what end?

Theorist Fredric Jameson has pointed to an important distinction between what he calls pastiche and parody:

> Pastiche is, like parody, the imitation of a peculiar
> or unique style . . . but it is a neutral practice of such
> mimicry . . . without the satirical impulse, without
> laughter, without that still latent feeling that there exists
> something normal compared to which what is being
> imitated is rather comic. Pastiche is blank parody, parody
> that has lost its sense of humor.[71]

In other words, pastiche happens when we lose our collective sense of a shared baseline. The satirizing continues, but we're cut adrift, unsure of whether laughter is the appropriate response considering the stakes. And since the satire often closely mirrors those in power, it's hard to know how we are shaming them. While it may have seemed like a tall order to shame George W. Bush, he at least kept up appearances—he was present at the White House Press Correspondents' Dinner, an event that Trump refused to even attend as president. There are ways in which comedy can provide a radical truth-telling, but it's just as common for comedians and satirists to traffic in cynicism.

Colbert's truth-telling performance at the Correspondents' Dinner provides an interesting contrast to the kind of comedy that came out of his regular TV show in which he continued to develop his right-wing talking-head character. "Language," Colbert said in a 2006 interview, "has always been important in politics, but language is incredibly important to the present political struggle . . . because if you can establish an atmosphere in which information doesn't mean anything, then there is no objective reality."[72]

Colbert was making a similar point to Jameson's. Political humor only has meaning if there's an accepted baseline of reality, and a generally agreed upon sense of what's reasonable: an understanding of how those in leadership positions *should* be behaving.

Which is a part of why his Correspondents' Dinner performance was so popular: His monologue relied on reminding us what a president should be doing, what the press should be doing. The scathing and cathartic humor lived in that distance between what our reality looked like versus what we had once understood it *should* look like.

But the parameters were different for his TV show. The problem, Colbert himself pointed out, is that the principle behind *The Colbert Report*—"what you wish to be true is all that matters, regardless of the facts"—was becoming the operating principle of those in our highest office of political leadership. As he puts it, "[A]t the time, we thought we were being farcical."[73]

Recall that just one year before the first episode of *The Colbert Report* aired on Comedy Central, journalist Ron Suskind published the now-famous quote from Karl Rove in *The New York Times Magazine*: "We're an empire now, and when we act, we create our own reality . . . and . . . all of you, will be left to just study what we do."

The question Colbert—and the rest of us—have had to reckon with since that time is what happens to intended farce when what seems farcical to you is the legitimate worldview of those in power.

What ends up happening is that your satire looks less like parodying and more like parroting.

IT WAS AROUND THE time of Colbert's scathing monologue— the second term of George W.—that we began to see comedians grappling with different strategies to satirize those in power. Take a 2008 *Daily Show* skit called "They're Trying to Kill Us," in which correspondent Jason Jones and Jon Stewart discuss the failure of oversight agencies such as the FAA, FDA, EPA, and mining agencies.

Stewart asks if there isn't a pattern emerging, and Jones comes back with a disturbing litany of examples: "Consider the facts: The 'response' to Hurricane Katrina, Christine Todd Whitman's false assurance there were no toxins at ground zero, numerous mining tragedies, the suppression of scientific facts supporting global warming, the failure to stop China from selling lead toys to America's children . . ." The exchange continues:

JON STEWART: It's incredible incompetence.

JASON JONES: Incompetence? Come on. If these people were truly this incompetent, they wouldn't be able to feed and clothe themselves, much less run agencies.

JS: What are you saying?

JJ: Jon, they're trying to kill us.

JS: Who?

JJ: The Bush administration!

JS: Why?

JJ: I don't know. Maybe they think it's funny, okay? Maybe they're trying to bring on the Rapture. Maybe Bush has to destroy the country in order to inherit his crazy uncle's fortune . . . Did you hear that?

JS: The crow? It's just a crow. You know we tape outside in a cemetery. Look, it's not like some ominous portent of death.

JJ: You're in on it. You're one of them.

JS: Don't be silly, Jason. This is just what happens when regulatory agencies are managed by the very people they're meant to regulate.

JJ: You're wearing a wire.

JS: It's a mic . . . so are you.

JJ: Oh god. Forget it. No more games, Stewart, if that is
your real name. *[Turns to camera]* The devastation that
this administration has wrought has to be deliberate.
Morons could never be this consistent. My eyes are wide
open now. What about you, Mr. and Mrs. America? Out
there in the audience, can you see? You gotta listen to
me. No matter where you are. They're going to get you.
On boltless planes, brakeless cars, shaftless mines, iceless
caps. Stay vigilant. They're coming for you.[74]

I remember the frustration I felt watching this sketch when
it aired. Here was Jason Jones's character providing a broader
framework, connecting the dots. It was a powerful and necessary
narrative, offering Americans a clear understanding of how fun-
damentally broken our regulatory agencies had become. And yet,
he's made out to be a madman while Jon Stewart offers up the
character we're meant to relate to: unsurprised, too smart to be
fooled, too savvy to be outraged. Meanwhile, Jones plays a par-
anoid conspiracy theorist—essentially for believing that what
has happened *has* actually happened. Instead of the facts of these
things carrying weight and leaving us concerned, we get to dismiss him as a lunatic. And so the tension that's built up over the
course of the sketch is diffused through laughter and dismissal of
Jones's madness.

We see this brand of cynical dismissal in Tina Fey's more
recent *SNL* appearance in the wake of the Charlottesville neo-
Nazi ("alt-right") rally. In a well-crafted rant, Fey points out the
absurdity of police firing rubber bullets at peaceful indigenous
protesters at Standing Rock while the neo-Nazis in Charlottesville were allowed to march through the streets carrying semi-

automatic weapons. Her litany about her disgust with what happened in Charlottesville grows until she offers up a solution: Buy a sheet cake, and eat it. Comfort food can make all of your worries go away. She begins shoveling cake into her mouth as she continues her rant. "Don't yell it at the Klan; yell it at the cake." Toward the end of the sketch, she says: "You start to feel powerless and that is when you need to dip a grilled cheese into the cake." At which point, she pulls a grilled cheese out from under the desk she's sitting at, and proceeds to dip the sandwich into the wreckage of cake and eat it.[75]

The morning after the sketch aired on *SNL*, my Facebook feed was flooded with friends who posted the video. "THIS," one friend wrote. And while I appreciated much of the humor in the sketch, I felt that familiar frustration of watching a well-known comedian deliver powerful material that ends with a punchline encouraging us to laugh the whole thing off or dig our heads in the sand (or sheet cake)—to count ourselves separate from the madness and grotesquerie that has emerged from our political leadership and the dregs of American culture.

It's no easy task to continue to find new ways to satirize those in power as they continue to behave in increasingly shameless ways. The problem is, comedians have become troublingly complicit: After months of Tina Fey playing Sarah Palin's character on *SNL*, Sarah Palin herself appeared on the show, taking the bite out of the satire by making it seem like she was in on the joke.[76] In 2015, *SNL* brought Trump on as a host after he'd announced his presidential bid—an unprecedented move for the show, which historically had invited presidential candidates to host only after they lost the primary or election.[77] During the 2016 campaign, Donald Trump also appeared on *The Tonight Show Starring Jimmy Fallon*, with Fallon famously ruffling the soon-to-be-president's hair while Trump got to play a good sport.[78] Less than a month after Trump's press secretary Sean Spicer resigned, he appeared in a sketch at the Emmy's alongside Stephen Colbert, mocking the lies he had peddled to Americans just weeks earlier by standing behind a podium and announcing to the Emmy audience: "This will be the largest audience to witness an Emmy's, period. Both in person, and around the world."[79]

What kind of laughter is this? As writer Jonathan Coe points out:

> "[T]he laughter which occasionally used to illuminate the dark corners of the political world with dazzling, unexpected shafts of hilarity has become an unthinking reflex on our part, a tired Pavlovian reaction to situations that are too difficult or too depressing to think about clearly."[80]

We laugh because it *used* to be funny and we don't seem to know what else to do in response to what's happening.

MANY OF THE COMEDIANS who regularly respond to daily news are doing the work of offering up narratives and frameworks that help us digest the glut of headlines and content that we encounter. In a society where we've hit an all-time low in our trust in mass media (higher only than our trust in big business and Congress),[81] these shows have filled a notable gap in our trusted-resources diet.

There are legitimate reasons for our loss of faith in journalism—especially as it's come to rely on an advertising-driven model. But there's something deeply troubling about the fact that many of us seem to trust, or at the very least rely on, satirists and comedians as much, if not more than, journalists. Their aims are often quite different, as are their responsibilities, but if they fail to recognize the gravity of the role they're playing, they can become—wittingly or not—complicit in the rise of someone like Trump.

Back in 2008, when asked about the monologue he delivered at the Correspondents' Dinner, Colbert insisted that he was there simply to "entertain," but he also seemed to recognize how the level of attention he was receiving for giving voice to the disdain and outrage so many Americans were feeling was a symptom of a much larger ailment. In a *New York* profile, he said: "It depresses me that there isn't a politician who can address that frustration that was clearly evident in the reaction to what I did. Where's the politician who can take advantage of that anger and that passion?"[82]

Colbert, Stewart, and a bevy of other comedians whose material relies on responding to the daily news have bristled at the implication that there should be more expected of them than that they provide entertainment. Colbert has said, "I'm not a political person, and I certainly don't have the answers."[83] Regardless of whether comedians want to be viewed as political or as generators of news or substantive analysis, they have come to functionally play that role.

If nothing else, the past fifteen years have seen a serious uptick in the blurring between entertainment, satire, and politics. When bumper stickers promoting "Stewart/Colbert '08" became popular, Stewart responded by saying, "Nothing says, 'I am ashamed of you, my government,' more than 'Stewart/Colbert '08.'"[84] While Stewart pointed to the deplorable state of confidence in our political system that he thought was revealed by those bumper stickers, it's also true that *Colbert ran for president* in 2007 after an outpouring of public enthusiasm and encouragement. He didn't end up being included on the ballot where he filed in his home state of South Carolina, but he insisted—in character—that he was serious about the run. In the end, it came down to a decision by the state's Democratic Party that he didn't meet the requirements: "that he be generally acknowledged as a viable nationwide candidate; and that he be actively campaigning for the state's primary."[85]

Apparently, it was a tough call: the chairwoman of the state's Democratic Party told *The New York Times*: "The council really agonized over this because they really like him, they love his show, and everyone thinks it's wonderful he cares about us."[86] Even those who are allegedly part of the news media seem to confuse the roles of journalist and satirist. In a 2004 appearance on CNN's *Crossfire*, Stewart told the show's host, Tucker Carlson, that he thought they staged fake debates and cheapened political discourse. Carlson counters that he thinks Stewart was too soft on John Kerry when he appeared on Stewart's show. "It's interesting to hear you talk about my responsibility," says Stewart. "I didn't realize that . . . the news organizations look to Comedy Central for their cues on integrity."[87]

It's a mic drop moment, but it's also a little humbling. Because, the fact is that we now *do* look to figures like Stewart for cues on integrity.

Thankfully, there are some signs that comedians are starting to recognize and embrace the powerful role they play in American politics. Alums of *The Daily Show* John Oliver and Samantha Bee launched their own shows in 2014 and 2016, respectively. They practice a slightly different approach than *The Daily Show* and *The Colbert Report*—a mash-up of standard jokes combined with substantive reporting and even solutions-oriented segments that highlight how Americans can take action. Their outrage, too, is closer to the surface. As is Colbert's in his newer role as host of

The Late Show. Here, Colbert has dropped the mimicking character act. He speaks as himself, often opening his show with a scathing to-camera monologue directed at Trump.

The most powerful segments in these shows often traffic in the same truth-telling approach, rooted in assertively pointing to where our collective baseline *should be*, and holding those in power accountable to it. One month into his presidency, Trump addressed Congress and managed to surprise much of the nation with a tone that was generally reasonable and conciliatory. Pundits weighed in by calling him "presidential," referring to it as an "extraordinary moment." It was the epitome of the bar having been lowered so far that Trump simply striking a presidential *tone* seemed miraculous. Samantha Bee responded on her show *Full Frontal* by combining a montage of pundits heaping praise on the president's speech before delivering a tirade: "What the fuck is wrong with you?! . . . If pundits set the bar for President Trump any lower, even Jeff Sessions won't be able to walk under it without bumping his head."[88]

Here, Bee was pointing directly to how pundits were normalizing Trump. In that same "presidential" speech, Trump also said, "It's a basic principle that those seeking to enter a country oughta be able to support themselves financially." Colbert hit back on *The Late Show* with: "Just like the [plaque on the] Statue of Liberty says, 'Give us your tired, your poor, but not so poor they can't afford a two-bedroom apartment and like, a Mitsubishi.'"[89] By pointing to the line of decency, and of what our standards and principles once were and *should be*, both Bee and Colbert engage in a truth-telling form of humor rather than a cynical dismissiveness.

THERE IS NO LONGER a clear dividing line between entertainers, satirists, and those in the "real" political playing field. At this point, we're wrestling with finding our way back to a shared baseline: What is it reasonable to expect from those in power? What is it reasonable to expect from those whose bread and butter is tied to analyzing and responding to the actions of those in power?

Trump emerged from—and exploited—a situation in which we are still actively grappling with these questions.

When demands for Trump to release his federal income tax returns before the election reached a fever pitch, Hillary Clinton tried to hold him accountable. During a debate, she pointed out that the only recent tax forms that were available showed that he didn't pay any federal income tax. Trump responded by saying, "That makes me smart."[90] Throughout his campaign, he continually bragged about things he got away with—from aggressively groping women without consent to not paying taxes to bribing politicians.[91]

Before Trump, Americans were well-versed in the corrupt politician, but we were still used to a certain kind of propriety—even if it was only lip service. Presidential candidates weren't meant to brag publicly about how they gamed the system because it spoke of their utter lack of regard for it, their cynicism for it. It was everyday Americans, entertainers, and satirists who held that privilege. We relied on the commander in chief to retain some semblance of earnestness so that we could maintain some faith in the system we relied on—to pave our roads, keep our water clean, educate us, and help us remain healthy. But Trump has engaged in a special kind of truth-telling—he's not a truth-teller in the vein of Diogenes because he has no interest in using his truth to hold those in power accountable. He's a truth-teller in that he boasts openly about using and abusing power to advance himself—and consolidate his own power—at every turn. He's simply the ultimate logical cynical conclusion to the trajectory we've been traveling. He's reflecting back to us our worst behaviors, and our utter contempt for politics.

Back in August 2006, halfway through George W. Bush's second term, Thomas Frank published a prescient *New York Times* editorial:

> [W]hat happens when you elevate to high public office people who actually . . . think that "the public interest" is a joke, that "reform" is a canard, and that every regulatory push is either a quest for monopoly by some company or a quest for bribes by some politician? What happens when the machinery of the state falls into the hands of people who laugh at the function for which it was designed? . . . What really worries me, though, is that our response to all this may be to burrow deeper into our own cynicism, ultimately reinforcing the gang that owns the patent on cynicism and thus setting us up for another helping of the same.[92]

It's a kind of terrifying complicity in which our cynicism— our continued default posture of having such a low regard for our political system and those who populate it—helps facilitate the rise to power of those who hold it in similarly low regard. As our trust in mass media has plummeted, we get a president who explicitly and vehemently attacks the press.

In his book *Cracking Up: American Humor in a Time of Conflict*, Paul Lewis writes that studies have shown that humor can "support denial and evasion, drawing observers . . . away from the urgent issues by enticing them to enjoy a little laugh about a subject and dismiss it from consciousness."[93] When we're joking about things that are so important, when events so relevant to policy decisions and Americans' well-being are being dramatized and satirized in a way that affirms the notion that we can't expect better from those in power, we risk losing a collective— and hugely necessary—moment of outrage. Instead, we cultivate a cynic's sneer.

There are ways in which the comedy world is doing incredible work to hold those in power accountable, and to remind us collectively of our standards for ethics and decency. Now, more than ever, we need them to recognize the importance of not perpetuating cynicism. It may sound like a high bar to hold comedians to, but as we've seen, they know how to deliver on this when they want to.

I think back to that Jason Jones sketch from 2008, and how the stakes have only intensified in the intervening years. We watched Jones's character devolving into madness, and the notion that the administration is "trying to kill us" was meant to seem absurd. Today, we have a president who has encouraged people at his rallies to "knock the crap" out of protesters,[94] who in response to a neo-Nazi rally that left one woman dead after a white supremacist drove a car into a crowd of protesters, insisted, "there is blame on both sides."[95] The heart of the conceit in the Jones sketch—"they're trying to kill us"—seems less and less like hyperbole. Our comedy has to evolve to keep up with our reality.

What if the sketch were tweaked so that the dark joke is that the paranoia turns out to be totally justifiable? In this reimagined sketch, instead of the comedic cop-out of having the punchline revolve around the weak joke of Jones being insane, we'd be led to the realization that it's mad *not* to recognize the reality of the conspiracy. At which point, Jon Stewart might join Jones in his now utterly reasonable paranoia. It's a different kind of humor—one that harkens back to the original definition of cynicism and its legacy of radical truth-telling. It might leave us in a state of discomfort, but I would argue that it has the potential to be as funny as, if not funnier than, the cheaper gag.

THE IMPORTANCE OF *NOW*

N SEPTEMBER OF 1945, INVESTIGATIVE journalist George Weller defied military orders and snuck into Nagasaki four weeks after Americans dropped an atomic bomb on the city. At the time, little was known about its radiation effects. The bombing was largely being lauded as the event that had helped put an end to the war. But when Weller visited hospitals in Nagasaki, he saw the horrific effects on civilians and came to understand that the story was much more complicated than what Americans understood. He wrote a series of articles about what he was seeing, but they were all intercepted by General Douglas MacArthur's censors and never made it to his editors back in the United States.[96]

Weller later wrote: "The moment when it could have been understood politically is missed, suppressed. The possibility of comprehension will never return again . . . The aim of well-timed censorship is to instill this simple idea: it probably never happened."[97]

It's a powerful notion and it makes intuitive sense: if we don't have the information we need to understand the magnitude of an event at the time it's happening, we lose our ability to become history's actors, to collectively reckon with the reality of an event, to respond and change course.

For every moment in history, there is an "event horizon"— a limited window of time to metabolize and respond to the information—after which the momentum of the moment is lost. But where Weller associated this with more straightforward censorship—which is still relevant today—there's another, more subtle way, that censorship occurs: if we're inundated with infor- mation and our attention is extremely fragmented, we're less able to process—or even identify—vital historical moments when they occur. Say a story about the Kardashians gets circulated as (or more) frequently as a story about revelations that confirm the Trump campaign conspired with Russian leadership in the lead-up to the 2016 election. If folks in the media think their job is to follow what's popular—what's being emailed or commented on the most—they'll dedicate as much or more time to the Kar- dashian story. The moment when we could collectively register outrage or concern passes amid the noise.

When we think about historical moments that had an impact, they tend to be events that interrupted our everyday lives with their magnitude. But events aren't inherently historical or impactful. Unless they happen in our backyards, news of them has to break through the noise so that we are all sitting up and paying attention.

Take the blurring of the lines between satire and reality, add to it the disaffected cynicism that we've all become steeped in, and you've got an equation for a brand of disbelief that can prevent us from finding our way to the kind of collective outrage that can lead to real change.

In a political era marked by daily scandals, it's important to parse the difference between surprise and outrage. So often, the default response to whatever the latest scandal is among those who follow the news is, "I'm not surprised." But not being surprised should not be synonymous with not being outraged. Think of it this way: If someone raped a single person, most of us would consider it an outrage. If that same person were to rape multiple people? It would be odd to respond in totality by saying, "I'm not surprised." And yet, that's precisely how so many of us respond to political scandal and corruption—a cynical dismissal and a commitment to counting ourselves apart, refusing to engage further.

The ability to be outraged, to recognize outrageous behavior when it occurs, is critical for our sense of reality, and for our safety. Without it, the general bar of what seems like reasonable behavior—rape culture, white supremacy, etc.—starts to lower. And without regularly flexing our collective outrage muscles, we start to experience a broad-based gaslighting as individuals— doubting the gravity of an event or transgression, even doubting our own eyes and sense of reality.

Take *Washington Post* reporter Ben Terris, who watched Trump campaign manager Corey Lewandowski violently push reporter Michelle Fields when she tried to ask Trump a question about affirmative action. This took place in early 2016, while Trump was still campaigning. When Terris reported on the event, the Trump campaign dragged him through the mud, denying that it happened so vehemently that Terris's editors questioned him repeatedly to verify the accuracy of his story.

"It happened right in front of me," Terris later wrote:

> In the moment, I was sure it happened . . . But by the time my editor asked me about it three days later, doubt had started to creep in. Trump had suggested Fields was probably making it up, and nobody else had corroborated my account. If it had really happened, Trump and his surrogates maintained, why wasn't there any footage?[98]

A few days later, the footage finally surfaced, confirming Terris's and Fields's accounts. It came as a relief to Terris, who had begun to question the truth of what he'd seen.

In May of 2017, Montana Republican Greg Gianforte pulled a similar maneuver, body slamming *Guardian* reporter Ben Jacobs (and breaking his glasses in the process) when he questioned Gianforte about the GOP health-care bill. Gianforte's campaign responded by releasing a statement claiming that Jacobs "aggressively shoved a recorder in Greg's face, and began asking badgering questions."[99] As though this was not simply a reporter doing his job. As though by doing his job, he was *asking for* or *deserved* this kind of violence.

These are just a couple examples of the kinds of episodes that may not be surprising to some, but that I would hope remain outrageous to most. The danger is that cynicism has become so pervasive in our culture that we are detached—so quick to not want to appear surprised or earnestly appalled by an event that we no longer have the space to generate outrage or even absorb the full gravity of the fact of it. We look the other way because we don't know how to metabolize the information or experience.

The Jon Stewart sketch that paints Jason Jones as an unhinged conspiracy theorist for pointing to observable reality raises the obvious question: In a society rife with outrageous actions undertaken by those in power, and conspiracies hiding in plain sight, what does it say that we paint those who point them out with the brush of madness?

If the Greek myth of Cassandra were rewritten for our current moment, she wouldn't even need to utter prophetic statements about the future to be dismissed. She'd merely need to state what was happening *right now* and so many of us either wouldn't hear her above the noise or would cross our arms and shrug, unsurprised.

IN GREECE, A YOUNG man named Manolis Glezos climbed the Acropolis as Nazi forces conquered Athens. It was 1941 and he and his friend—both eighteen years old at the time—went on foot, carrying only a knife and lantern. Together, they tore down and destroyed the Nazi flag, an act Glezos was imprisoned and tortured for. He decided not to learn his lesson and ,after the war was over, continued to actively oppose the right-wing government that had supported the Nazis. That earned him multiple death sentences before he was eventually pardoned. While in prison, he was elected to Parliament. Now in his nineties, Glezos is still a regular figure on the frontlines of protests in Greece and has served as a member of Parliament a number of times. He recently told writer Bill Ayers:

> I'm interested in people collectively discovering their own
> power . . . The biggest obstacle to revolution here—and
> I'll bet it's true in your country as well—is a serious and

often unrecognized lack of confidence. We spend our lives
in the presence of mayors and governors and presidents
and chiefs of police, and then we lose our power of self-
reliance, and we doubt that we could live without those
authorities . . . we may not mean to but . . . soon enough
we embrace our own passivity and become enslaved to a
culture of obedience.[100]

There's something so intoxicating in the simplicity with which
Glezos asserts that we all have power, and he's right. But this resistance to recognizing and acknowledging our power goes beyond
authority worship or lack of confidence in ourselves. The fact is,
there's comfort in refusing to recognize our potential and our
power. To do so is to immediately reckon with our responsibility and our complicity. As disempowering as it may be to feel like
we're only spectators to a dismal political process, it can be down-
right paralyzing to think that we are in any way *responsible* for how
dismal the political situation has become.

But this desire to stand apart, to identify as observers rather
than participants, is precisely what brought us president Trump. I
don't mean to imply that it is solely American citizens' responsibility. There are powerful moneyed interests that are gerrymandering
the hell out of our country, carving it up into some of the most
abstract shapes you'll see this side of Kandinsky, all in an effort to
take away the power of our votes. There is an antiquated electoral
college system in place that skews the weight of votes from different states. And that's just one tip of one iceberg among many.

But the distance we've put between our core beliefs and our
political system is what has allowed it to be hijacked by cynical
power brokers who view it as a game to be rigged in order to continue accumulating their own personal power and wealth. The risk

is in accepting their cynical perspective of our system by mirroring it—responding as though those in power who are working against the concerns of the majority of Americans are only behaving as they are supposed to.

In our desire to keep our hands clean, to not be complicit, we end up disenfranchising ourselves, stripping ourselves of what power we might have. We stand back, watching the ship slowly sinking with folded arms, comforting ourselves with the knowledge that we knew all along the ship would sink, while avoiding acknowledging that *we're on the same damn ship*.

Right now, we face an unenviable reality: one in which many of those with the power to shape the national dialogue and our sense of who we are as Americans have abandoned their posts. We're left with the burden of having to fiercely push forward our own narratives and our own sense of reality. We're at a vital crossroads where we either accept the cynical narratives echoed by much of the media, or hold tight to what we know to be true—that we want and need leadership that speaks to the better angels of our nature.

There's a reason many of us feel lost and overwhelmed: so many of the narratives we're being offered to explain our collective reality are outdated. They fly in the face of history and who we know ourselves to be. It's time for journalists and pundits to examine their responsibilities, and the role they wish to play in a democracy that has gone off the rails. The story of American democracy isn't a story whose ending is already written. We can't wait for it to be written *for us*. We must write it ourselves and break through the noise by counting ourselves in, by engaging with our political system, running for office, joining protests in the streets, calling our representatives, and showing up at their offices—however pointless we're told these vital actions are. The degree to which we push forward with our own narratives and write the story for ourselves is the degree to which we can salvage our sense of ourselves and our democracy. Political writer and researcher Michael Signer has said that:

> Demagogues thrive when we're cynical about truth. They start to deflate when we put faith back again in public reason, and if you look at the history, we have always prevailed. And it's not the checks and balances that we have . . . it's because the American people in the end always choose that demagogues are beneath them.[101]

Choosing that demagogues are beneath us requires that we move beyond the defensive savviness we know too well into the uncomfortable realm of envisioning, hoping, and trying. There will most certainly be failure along the way, but there is no way in which the failure can be more spectacular than what will happen if we continue to watch passively as cynics hijack our democracy, all the while blaming us for the violence and destruction they've set in motion.

Choosing that demagogues are beneath us requires us to view ourselves as powerful and recognize the necessity of using that power. It's a question of survival.

ON OBJECTIVITY

I may not have always been satisfactorily balanced;

I always tended to argue that objectivity was

of less importance than truth.

—JAMES CAMERON, BRITISH JOURNALIST[1]

What would happen if one woman told the truth about

her life? The world would split open.

—MURIEL RUKEYSER, POET[2]

OUR SEXUAL PREDATOR IN CHIEF

WAS ON A BUS IN New York, headed upstate. It was night-time and the lights had been turned off—the only sounds the oceanic ebb and flow of passing cars and the occasional grunt from a sleeping passenger. Still, when I saw the breaking headline come up on the screen of my phone, I couldn't help myself. I whooped. I turned to my friend dozing in the seat next to me, shout-whispering: *Grab them by the pussy! There's no way he can recover from that.* It was a month before the election and an outtake of a conversation between Donald Trump and Billy Bush from a 2005 episode of *Access Hollywood* had just gone viral. "I did try and fuck her . . ." Trump can be heard saying about a woman. "I moved on her like a bitch . . ."[3]

Of course, I was deeply wrong. Trump *did* recover.

TWO WEEKS AFTER THE election, I heard from my friend M. She was upset. She wanted to tell me about something that happened to her more than a decade ago, when a group of young men groped her in a crowd while she was traveling. "I've occasionally told that story," she explained, "but I just told it like it was a crazy travel story." At the time it had happened, she said, she was shaken, but made her way back to her hotel room and just chalked it up to a lousy day. After seeing the *Access Hollywood* video, after watching it fail to affect the outcome of the election, M.'s narrative shifted. "For the first time ever," she said, "I realized that I was sexually assaulted."

M. wept as she experienced what she described as "the all-too-familiar feeling of humiliation."

I hated that she felt the humiliation belonged to her, a thing she was tasked with holding instead of its rightful owners—the men who had behaved in a way that revealed the shortcomings of their own humanity.

I hated it all the more because I knew I held the same humiliation myself. It was not only the humiliation of having had numerous encounters in which I was belittled, harassed, assaulted, or otherwise treated as lesser-than because of my perceived gender or race.

Like M., I found myself suddenly revisiting experiences from the past—recognizing how I had worked to excuse, minimize, justify, or utterly rewrite them. The humiliation came from recognizing my complicity in this reshaping and rewriting.

THAT TRUMP VIDEO HAUNTS M. and it haunts me. Not only because it features our now-president bragging about sexual predation. What pains me just as much is what happens *after* Trump boasts about grabbing women by the pussy: As his bus approaches its destination, we see soap opera actress Arianne Zucker standing in a parking lot, waiting to greet Trump before his cameo on her show, *Days of Our Lives*. Bush and Trump catch sight of her from the bus and begin discussing how great her legs are, at which point Trump says, "I'm gonna use some Tic Tacs just in case I start kissing her." Then he goes on to deliver his famous line: "You know I'm automatically attracted to beautiful—I just start kissing them. It's like a magnet. Just kiss. I don't even wait. And when you're a star, they let you do it. You can do anything. Grab them by the pussy. *I can do anything.*"

I can do anything.

When Trump and Bush get off the bus, they organize themselves into the semblance of respectability, straighten their suit jackets, and greet Zucker as if they had not just been discussing her as though she were a fetching cut of meat. Zucker greets them with a handshake. "Are you ready to be a soap star?" she says. But Bush doesn't seem to be able to shift gears to professional mode. "How about a little hug for the Donald," he says. "He just got off the bus"—as though this were a feat worthy of reward. Zucker awkwardly reaches over and hugs Trump. As they walk to the set, Zucker starts to explain to Trump how their upcoming scene will go. With Bush and Trump flanking her, Bush interrupts to ask, "Now, if you had to choose honestly between one of us, me or the Donald . . . seriously, if you had to take one of us as a date."

Here's the part where I flinch, look away from the screen: "I'm gonna have to take the fifth on that one," she says, nervous laughter bubbling in her throat. "Really?" Bush says. Zucker corrects herself in a rush, "I'll take both," she says.

I knew that laugh, that attempt to placate. I know it so well, it made me blush to watch. *That all-too-familiar feeling of humiliation.* When I hear that kind of laughter, I imagine all the laughter shaped by the force of women's discomfort or fear. I imagine all of it accruing over centuries in a bottle that might someday come uncorked, our ears ringing at its deafening cacophony.

It was a similar humiliation my friend M. felt when she tried to minimize her experience of being assaulted, willing a different shape onto the narrative—one in which the experience could be a tidy travel anecdote, one in which it could all be laughed off. It was similar to the humiliation I felt at my friend's Thanksgiving gathering just two weeks after Trump was declared president. As the men around the table began their discussion about "whether women are as funny as men," I was confronted with the complexity of the human I was, suddenly reduced to the assumed essentialism of my gender. The quickening of my pulse, the rage that I believed I had to stifle—an internal voice seemingly delivered from the most primitive, survival-steeped part of my brain: *Don't let them know it upset you.* The reining in of fear and frustration, the bark of laughter like some lurch at reclaiming what little power and dignity I thought might be left to me.

After the election, I wondered at that distant but familiar compulsion: to stay cool, to not reveal my fear, shock, and rage. How much it reminded me of being a teenage girl—laughing along when a boy I barely knew joked about putting his dick in my mouth or calmly continuing to sharpen my pencil at school even as my eye caught my name followed by "is a slut" graffitied in small perfect letters on the wall in front of me. At what age do we master that skill—of hiding our selves beneath an increasingly well-rehearsed veneer of unaffectedness?

I found myself in a state of self-loathing. I hated that I seemed to be reverting to that younger self. I didn't want to diminish my rage, didn't want to laugh knowingly.

I understood that if there were ever a time to push back, to let my rage be seen and felt, it was in the weeks after Trump's election. Already, there had been a profound uptick in hate crimes across the country. I began to eye people I once would have presumed were allies, unsure of whether I could feel safe with them, whether they believed in the full extent of my humanity.

I was, like many other female, brown, queer, and immigrant folks I knew, more scared when I went out into the world. More watchful, more cautious. More inclined to have my fight-or-flight impulse triggered by a conversation at a dinner party. At the same time, I felt more responsible for holding the line, for speaking up (when it felt safe to), for fear that if I didn't, that line would slide decades into the past. But I was also up against that deeply visceral sensation: that my survival relied on keeping myself small, agreeable.

In the back of a cab on my way home from that Thanksgiving dinner, I steadied my breathing. I was working to achieve the calmness that it had just taken so much effort to perform. I heard the ding of my phone, and saw my friend had texted to say that the man who had most directly engaged me with the question of whether women were as funny as men had said this when I left: "She's a very smart lady." *Smart. For a lady.*

I fought off a wave of nausea. What had felt to me like a conversation about my very worth and humanity was to him a brief chapter of amusing dinner discussion.

Like my friend M., like Zucker, I was left holding the shame and humiliation of the moment. Compounding that, I felt complicit, because I had tried to laugh it off, to diminish my shock and outrage. I did it because I felt powerless. Or, rather, I was so steeped in the narrative of powerlessness that I resorted to playing a role that was as familiar as it was impossibly uncomfortable.

OBJECTIVELY SPEAKING

IN THE WAKE OF THE election, when I felt that urgent need to *do something*, the intuitive move was to use my skills as a writer and journalist to respond. And yet the fear and anger I was experiencing didn't have a home in the kind of writing I was accustomed to doing.

For most of my career, I had approached my work from what I liked to believe was a place of objectivity. That I was a brown woman was evident to me and anyone I interacted with. I have never tried to hide this identity, but it's true that I also never led with it, or implied publicly that it had a significant bearing on my perspective. I had supported my brothers and sisters in their feminist and anti-racist work. I had occasionally protested alongside them. I had put my money where my mouth is, but I had not as often used that mouth directly.

I have always kept something of a distance from confronting and tackling "personal" or "identity" issues head-on. Where my colleagues were willing to closely examine the dregs of humanity—from the men's rights movement to white supremacists—I tended to work at more of a remove. I cut my teeth as a journalist during the George W. Bush administration, reporting on the legal arguments used to justify the use of torture in the "war on terror," the ins and outs of corporate manipulation of the system, from Enron to Amazon. I was concerned with questions of justice and equality, but I rarely addressed misogyny and racism head-on.

My justification went like this: To acknowledge the arguments of people who thought I was lesser-than for being brown or a woman was a net loss. It meant ceding the terms of the discussion in some way. It meant acknowledging that I was listening to them.

As a journalist, my outsider stance was a convenient excuse, dovetailing nicely with my aversion to calling too much attention to my identity. Raised by a white mother who encouraged me—beautifully, naively—to believe I could be, and accomplish, anything I chose to, I tended toward obliviousness (sometimes willful; sometimes unintentional) when I encountered misogyny and racism. Being well-educated and relatively light-skinned, I was able to move with more ease through circles that may have alienated or rejected others who were more visibly "other."

What I was trying to do was pass. As neutral. As objective. I thought the way to do this was by avoiding any mention of what were "personal" traits, such as my brownness and femaleness. I thought I might strip myself of them.

But it only left me groping in the dark when I encountered situations to which my obliviousness rendered me illiterate.

In one of my first jobs after college, I worked as an editor at a progressive news publication. I wrote articles most weekends, but I was not paid for them. It was an arrangement that I didn't question until a male coworker mentioned to me that he really appreciated the additional income he received from writing articles off the clock. My first thought was: *Oh, my articles must not be good enough to warrant compensation.*

It was compensation I sorely needed. In order to support myself, I worked evenings as a cocktail waitress, going straight from the publication's San Francisco offices to a bar up in the wealthy neighborhood of North Beach. For that gig, I wore the standard uniform: a pair of snug black pants and a black shirt. I realize now that I made sure I never wore anything form-fitting to the office. At the end of the work day, I would change out of my shapeless clothing—drawstring pants, shirts purchased a size or two up—in the office bathroom. I don't think I even fully acknowledged that the reason behind this—and my choice of clothing at the office more generally—was because I did everything I could to avoid any notice from my boss. I put so much energy into trying to be viewed by him solely as a disembodied brain—an attempt to escape the behaviors I had seen him display with other women, from compliments on outfits to a predilection for starting conversations about their sex lives. The idea of him even being aware that I possessed a body, or a sexuality of any kind, was terrifying to me.

Weeks after I learned from my male coworker that he was being paid for his off-the-clock-articles, I drummed up the nerve to ask my boss for a raise. I cringe to think of how much time I spent preparing, perusing books with titles like *How to Negotiate a Raise*, calling more experienced friends for tips. When the meeting finally took place, I carefully laid out my case—citing the volume of work I was producing and its popularity among readers. He disarmed me in seconds. Smiling with a kind of coy concern, my fifty-something-year-old white male boss asked me, "Are you having trouble paying rent? How much do you need?" I didn't understand how the conversation had shifted so quickly from being about compensation for my work to him becoming some kind of savior or sugar daddy, doing me a personal favor. When I tried to right the conversation by asserting that it wasn't about my rent, he became angry and dismissive. I did not get the raise.

My head would spin after encounters like this. But because I was steeped in the narrative of meritocracy (and its subtext of color- and gender-blindness), of hard work yielding just returns, I didn't have the framework to understand the full picture of what was happening. I was left carrying stories like this alone, attributing them to some personal shortcoming. It was remarkably easy to blame myself.

What I didn't understand at the time was that by not placing my experiences within the broader framework of institutional sexism and racism, by not seeking out readily available stories that closely resembled my own, I was doing myself a disservice. I was contributing to a broader atomizing force that stymies any possibility of change or revolution: I was throwing myself on the altar of "I" when I should have been adding my voice to an already well-established "we." Over a decade later, I would learn just how much it had cost me—and many others—to follow this path when a group of current and former employees came together during the #metoo movement. Over a series of emails in which we all shared our experiences, we came to realize the scope of our former boss's abusive behavior. Every one of us had endured varying degrees of it—ranging from unwanted attention, touching, and harassment to outright sexual coercion. Few of us had realized how systematic these abuses were.

Mirroring a kind of cynical posture, I held myself apart from the realities of bigotry and misogyny. I tried to count myself out. I was operating under the unexamined and mistaken hope that, if I simply refused to acknowledge reality, I would somehow avoid it. As though I could escape being subjected to the same treatment as my peers.

Of course, there's a reason that we cling to these narratives of objectivity, equality, and meritocracy. There's a real comfort to them. They are stirring and laudable goals woven deep in the fabric of America. But it's a tricky threadwork: Those with more privilege tend to see in it the pattern of a promise already fulfilled. Those reminded daily of how the system is rigged, a hollow promise or a promise betrayed.

At either end of this spectrum, there can be a powerful dissociation: a sense that this country's promises—whether fulfilled or unfulfilled—are a done deal. Instead of thinking of America as an ongoing experiment, one in which we are vital actors, one which we have the agency and responsibility to reshape, too many of us hunker down in this understanding of America as a static space, immutable. We adapt and adjust to situations that urgently demand of us that we instead practice a robust maladjustment.

OBJECTIVITY AND JOURNALISM

AS A JOURNALIST, ONE OF the assumed cardinal rules of the trade is to *be objective*. But as soon as we try to define what that means, things get complicated.

During the heyday of the "war on terror," when the Bush administration promoted the use of torture in Guantanamo as well as other military bases and black sites around the world, many major news outlets dropped the ball in the name of objectivity. Despite the fact that the historical record shows that torture does not lead to useful or reliable information—and that it is illegal under both national and international law—publications repeatedly cranked out articles quoting Bush administration officials who claimed it *did* work and *was* legal, often giving equal air time and column inches to both perspectives as though they were similarly rooted in fact and deserving of our consideration. This approach had the effect of legitimizing the notion that this was a valid debate.

It's a concept that has a name, "fairness bias," whereby journalists or publications are so preoccupied with the appearance of balance that they give equal time to opposing perspectives, even if one is less valid or patently untrue.[4] This false objectivity also promotes the intellectually lazy tendency to find two sides to a story, even if there are twelve, and then give equal space to each. But if someone—no matter how much power they have—is saying things that are categorically false or misleading, to simply publish their quotes or perspective without clearly placing them in the context of their lack of grounds or the falseness of their claims is deeply misleading.

Fairness bias shares some similarities with the "status-quo bias," which media critic Andrew Cline describes as the mainstream media's tendency to "never question the structure of the political system."[5] We see this in the tendency of reporters to cover political races in a top-down manner, following the ins and outs of what the Democratic and Republican candidates are saying and doing as the overarching framework rather than letting the concerns and issues of Americans drive the election coverage.

This bias reached peak levels during the coverage of Trump's campaign and immediately after the election, which had the effect of normalizing a political race that was anything but normal. In a meeting Trump had with *The New York Times* two weeks after the election, a reporter asked about climate change. He framed it in a context Trump might understand: that he owned "some of the most beautiful . . . golf courses in the world." In his response, Trump rambled about how the hottest day ever was actually in "1890 something," how his uncle was an engineer at MIT, how a lot of smart people disagree with the fact that climate change is actually happening, and he's "not sure anybody is ever going to really know" whether it's happening.[6] Thus ended the hard-hitting inquiry.

The transcript of the softball conversation was disturbing to read. Who was setting the parameters here? By publishing the full text of the conversation, the *Times* was likely trying to find ways to circumvent Trump's ongoing accusations that the media lies, misquotes, or otherwise distorts his words. *Give him enough rope and he'll hang himself.* But this mistakenly assumes that Trump actually cares about veracity.

There's an even subtler manifestation of fairness bias: I call it the "underplaying bias"—the tendency of journalists to under-play the gravity of a situation in order to not appear alarmist or prejudiced. In a February 2017 headline, *The New York Times* published an article about the Trump administration's bigoted travel ban under the headline "Justice Dept. Says a Ban on Travel Is Vital to Safety."[7] Compare that with *Slate*'s "The New Travel Ban Is an Abomination,"[8] written by legal scholar Dahlia Lith-wick, or with *The Washington Post*'s "With Trump Travel Ban Stay, Immigrants Scramble to Get Back to U.S."[9] The tone and focus drastically alter how readers understand the stakes.

The question of how to responsibly frame issues is one I often turned my attention to when I was covering the Bush adminis-tration's policy of promoting the use of torture: Would a journal-ist be going too far when reporting the illegal policy of torture to simply call it "illegal"? What refreshing candor for such an article to be printed on the front page, under a headline that made the stakes clear rather than assuaging concerns or putting readers to sleep with its banal dailiness. Consider "Some concerns expressed about war on terror policy" versus "President's torture policies violate law." Or, take a January 2018 article in *The New York Times*: initially headlined "Republicans See Child Health Plan as a Bargaining Chip," the language was soon changed to "G.O.P. to Use Children's Health Insurance as Lure for Averting Shutdown"—an injection of more convoluted and dull language ostensibly used in an attempt to soften the framing and appear more "balanced," despite the story explicitly detailing a Republican attempt to use a vote to continue health insurance coverage for 9 million children as a bargaining chip.[10]

These often unconscious biases don't just impact and affect readers' perspectives. Journalists who don't examine their tendency to engage in fairness and underplaying biases may end up doubting their own grasp on reality. It's that kind of blindness that led reporter Ben Terris to question whether he had actually witnessed Trump's campaign manager violently push a reporter, even though, as he said, "[i]t happened right in front of me."[11]

When Donald Trump was running for president, many journalists made the faulty assumption that someone like him didn't possess the legitimacy to make it to the Oval Office. Once he was elected, it was as though they compounded that failure by pursuing another faulty line of logic: since he won, they had to legitimize him.

The way numerous journalists covered his campaign as though it was business as usual went beyond simple sycophantism; it was an irrational faith in the game. Writer Masha Gessen covered the rise of Vladimir Putin for years, and she issued alarm bells throughout Trump's campaign. Gessen pointed to the way many journalists slavishly narrated every move as though it were a chess game, instead of taking a step back and acknowledging that Trump was busy knocking all the figures off the board. "Well, just say it," Gessen entreated. "Just say he was not playing chess!"[12]

This refusal to accept or acknowledge that the rules had been rendered moot is precisely what bestowed Trump with legitimacy. Gessen has also made the case that we need to become more comfortable with using "big, scary words"—words like "fascist," "racist," or "Nazi"—when appropriate. Not doing so has detrimental effects, preventing us "from seeing just how dire a threat Trump is"—and how recognizable his tactics are when we examine other autocratic leaders from history.[13] We see this aversion to using appropriate words from history in everything from the media peddling the euphemistic term "alt-right" in lieu of the white nationalist or neo-Nazi movement, to everyday Americans quibbling over whether or not it's fair to call Trump racist. And while we argue about whether or not that thing with the many wheels conveyed on a track is actually a train, the thing has already left the station.

We rely on journalists and those in power to give context to and affirm what we're observing, to take the pulse of the collective. It's what allows us to identify actionable moments—those limited windows before the "event horizons"—when outrage has the potential to go beyond the individual and become a part of a larger collective moment that carries promise for real change.

In a political era marked by numerous scandals, more journalists need to do the job that political comedy shows have taken on by default: placing a single occurrence within a broader narrative rather than offering up each instance piecemeal. The former approach allows us to connect the dots, building toward outrage when it's appropriate and necessary to maintaining our democracy. The latter feeds a kind of fragmentation, contributing to a sense that each of these incidences of corruption is unrelated to the others—even in situations where there are clear ties. Without a more cohesive narrative, these constant, individual stories of malfeasance promote a different narrative: that *everyone* in power is corrupt, that it makes sense for us to be cynical—to believe this behavior is simply all we can expect.*

In the absence of an open and in-depth public conversation about what terms like "objectivity" and "neutrality" actually mean, and how they should be practiced, they are often wielded in ways that perpetuate a false objectivity. Whether it's a journalist self-censoring to strike a "reasonable" or "objective" tone, or managers policing reporters with unwritten rules about what constitutes objectivity, the end result is that reporters are often actively discouraged from having and providing perspectives that could help Americans understand what's happening to our democracy—both the scope and stakes. The arbitrary and ever-shifting definitions of what constitutes an "objective" tone leaves us with a reality in which the prevailing subjective notions of the time are passed off as a kind of capital-O objectivity.

ON OCTOBER 15, 2011, during the heart of the Occupy Wall Street movement, Caitlin Curran, a freelance reporter for *The Takeaway* (co-produced by Public Radio International and WNYC), and her boyfriend attended a march to Times Square.

---

* It's worth mentioning that journalism tends to have a "problem bias" more broadly. In other words, coverage is often so fixated on cataloguing and exposing the problems in our political and social realms that there's a tendency to give short shrift to—or utterly ignore—what citizens and politicians are doing to counteract or respond to the problems. Without a more solutions-oriented journalism, it takes greater effort to be engaged and effective citizens.

They had brought along a handmade sign featuring an adapted quote from *Atlantic* writer Conor Friedersdorf: "It's wrong to create a mortgage-backed security filled with loans you know are going to fail so that you can sell it to a client who isn't aware that you sabotaged it by intentionally picking the misleadingly rated loans most likely to be defaulted upon." It was a physically hefty sign that Curran's boyfriend wanted a break from holding. So, for a moment, Curran took over, and someone took her picture. The photo made the rounds on the internet, and when her bosses came across the image, Curran was fired.[14]

Lisa Simeone, an independent contractor for NPR, was similarly fired when the organization learned that she had helped organize an Occupy Wall Street–related protest in Washington, D.C.[15] These incidents demand that we grapple with a few vital questions: At what point do reporters sacrifice their supposed "neutrality" and "objectivity" in a way that renders them unfit for their jobs? And, what does it mean for their sense of responsibility as humans and citizens to be at odds with their responsibility as journalists?

The rise of social media, too, has upped the ante. In October 2017, *The New York Times* issued new guidelines for staff journalists' use of their private social media accounts, insisting that they "should be especially mindful of appearing to take sides on issues that the *Times* is seeking to cover objectively." The guidelines also forbid journalists from joining any "secret" groups on Facebook or other platforms "that may have a partisan orientation," explicitly stating that journalists "should also refrain from registering for partisan events on social media." The lengthy list of restrictions concludes with the advice that if reporters remain uncertain, "ask yourself . . . Would you express similar views in an article on the *Times*'s platforms?"[16] Perhaps most extreme: they issued similar guidelines for freelance contract workers.[17] In this case, the quest for objectivity is so rabid, it constitutes censorship.

If we want journalists to be working on behalf of everyday Americans, does it make sense to restrict their ability to go where the stories are? If journalists are fixated on avoiding any behavior that can be seen as partisan—even in their private lives—what kind of impact does that have on the type and quality of the stories they then publish? How in touch are they likely to be with the concerns of the citizenry if they cannot be engaged citizens themselves?

Both Simeone and Curran were participating in protests that framed problematic aspects of our reality: Americans were losing their homes because banks had colluded against them. There is a huge gap in income between 99 percent of Americans and the wealthiest 1 percent. These aren't just academic topics. They relate to deeply personal and political questions regarding the ability of the vast majority of Americans—including Simeone and Curran themselves—to be able to afford a roof over their heads and obtain health care without going bankrupt in the process.

What does it mean when even acknowledging these basic facts is deemed problematically political—enough to be considered a fireable offense?

We want to have confidence in our journalists—confidence that they are examining all available facts, that they are conveying the scope and stakes of the situation, that they don't have some extremist partisan agenda. But what if the reporter who examines all the available facts comes to the conclusion that Americans are being screwed over? Doesn't journalists' ability to say as much speak to their integrity and trustworthiness rather than a dereliction of duty?

These kinds of questions are urgently important to explore, which is why I was encouraged when I saw *Marketplace* reporter Lewis Wallace's blog post just ten days after Trump was sworn in as president. In it, Wallace called into question whether the way we practice neutrality and objectivity as journalists is ethical and functional. His desire to probe these questions was rooted in the personal:

> As a member of a marginalized community (I am transgender), I've never had the opportunity to pretend I can be "neutral." After years of silence/denial about our existence, the media has finally picked up trans stories, but the nature of the debate is over whether or not we should be allowed to live and participate in society, use public facilities and expect not to be harassed, fired or even killed. Obviously, I can't be neutral or centrist in a debate over my own humanity.[18]

How does one cover outright hatred and bigotry objectively or neutrally?

Two hours after posting his reflections, Wallace received a call from his boss saying that it was in violation of *Marketplace*'s ethics code. He was subsequently fired. He published a follow-up piece on *Medium*, reporting on what had happened and making it clear why he wanted to share his story with the public:

> I know I'm not the only one having doubts about our role as journalists. I hope I can contribute to a meaningful conversation about how media organizations need to change to adapt to the times, putting ethics and morality into historical context—history shows these things change as politics shift. I have been told a few times that this is a simple choice between "journalism" and "activism." I believe my original piece makes clear why I find that binary to be false.

Wallace *did* try to push back. But when he asked how, exactly, his personal post had violated his employers' policies, he was told it was because *Marketplace* believed in objectivity and neutrality. Because neither of these terms were defined (or even articulated) in its code of ethics, it was left up to his boss to arbitrarily dictate their meaning.

After reading about Wallace's firing, I immediately thought of WNYC spokesperson Jennifer Houlihan's defense of their decision to fire Curran for attending an OWS protest. "When Ms. Curran made the decision to . . . make herself part of the story, she violated our editorial standards."[19]

But wasn't she *already* part of the story?

Like Wallace, I've come to realize that we do violence to ourselves, others, and our country when we do not admit to our subjectivity, to the particularity of our experiences. When we presume there is no place for our actual backgrounds, identities, concerns, needs, and desires in politics. In an attempt to perform an objective or neutral voice, we censor ourselves. We become complicit with a system that allows the question of our humanity to remain up for debate. What we need now is a journalism that does not pit "objectivity" against basic humanity. When reporters prioritize the stakes a policy or politicians' agenda has for the majority of Americans or for specific populations that will be most impacted, we get not only a more ethical journalism, but one that makes us all more informed and effective citizens.

DEFAULT OBJECTIVITY

IN GRAD SCHOOL, I TOOK a literature class with a focus on colonialism. My professor, Gitanjali Shahani, was always bringing primary resources to class, often jaw-dropping early texts from the British Empire. One text in particular stood out: "Boorde's Illustrated Guide to People Published in 1542," during the nascent days of British empire-building.[20] At the start of the first chapter is an image of a white male in his skivvies, armed with a pair of scissors. These, the author notes, were for the Englishman to make clothing from the fabrics of the world. Included at the front was a poem describing the guide's conceit:

> I am an English man, and naked I stand here,
> Musyng in my mynde what raiment I shal were;
> For now I wull were thys, and now I wyl were that;
> Now I wyl were I cannot tel what.
> All new fashyons be plesaunt to me;
> I wul haue them, whether I thryue or thee.
>
> I do feare no man; all men feryth me;
> I ouercome my aduersaries by land and by see.

The idea was that being a white male subject of the British Empire offered the privilege of neutrality. You could "try on" the ethnicities of the world—becoming a dark-skinned Moor with "great lips and knotted hair" or a "light-fingered" Egyptian. You could try on something else because you were a blank canvas—you could become and do whatever you pleased because, as a white man, you were invested with no other innate qualities. Except, of course, supremacy over anyone who was not a white man.

I was reminded of Boorde's guide when Justice Sonia Sotomayor was going through the Supreme Court confirmation process in 2009. She had come under fire for stating that being a woman and Latina influenced her perspective.

"I think the system is strengthened when judges don't assume they're impartial," she testified, "but [rather] when judges test themselves to identify when their emotions . . . or their experiences are driving their results."[21]

Senator Jeff Sessions of Alabama, now the US attorney

general, agitatedly adjusted his glasses and responded, "Aren't you saying . . . that you expect your background and heritage to influence your decision-making . . . ? [Y]ou accept that there may be sympathies, prejudices and opinions that legitimately can influence a judge's decision?" Sessions remarked: "I reject such a view, and Americans reject such a view."[22]

I was troubled by that slippery slope between "I" and "Americans" that Sessions traveled in a single breath. I mulled it over for days before I recognized why the statement had lodged itself like a splinter beneath my skin: implicit in Sessions's reaction was a presumption that his perspective was objective and American in a way that Sotomayor's perspective was not.

How impossible a situation: you are raised in a country where you're socialized differently, treated as "other," and then chastised for acknowledging this fact.

And how odd that acknowledging that human beings are not inherently objective—that their perspectives are shaped by their experiences of the world—is so objectionable to Sessions. Here, Sotomayor was articulating the real work of approaching neutrality and objectivity. She was acknowledging her experiences and examining their impact on her perspective in order to "test" herself. This is the same kind of work required of any human being who strives toward self-awareness and self-knowledge. It's akin to the definition of objectivity that philosopher and linguist Noam Chomsky aspires to in his own work, saying, "I also try, particularly in political writing, to make it extremely clear in advance exactly where I stand so that readers can make judgments accordingly. The idea of neutral objectivity is at best misleading and often fraudulent."[23]

Sessions's response perfectly encompasses white privilege: the presumption that your subjective way of being in and seeing the world constitutes a uniquely objective perspective. We cannot discuss our received notions of objectivity without recognizing that they are commonly located in this default white male perspective. What we tend to think of as objectivity is actually a very particular subjectivity run amok.*

LIKE MOST AMERICANS, I was raised to be a white man: I read William Faulkner and Ernest Hemingway. I read F. Scott Fitzgerald and Charles Bukowski. I came to identify with the emotionally disengaged characters, the staccato sentences, the irreverent dirty old man voice. The books I read asked me to imagine the power I might have. I got women pregnant and then worried that they wouldn't get an abortion, tying me down forever when all I wanted to do was continue experiencing my freedom. I wrote poems about the absurdity of writing poems, enjoying the decadence of imagining my readers drinking in my disregard for them. Being likeable, explaining oneself to others, were not prerequisites of protagonism. I watched women move—their hips in dresses, their lips on glasses, their breasts heaving. All of it offered up to me, to enjoy, to consume. The fact that I was a brown woman was not something that seemed immediately relevant when I was younger.

I moved through the world with this sense that I would have access to the same kind of power as the protagonists of the books I read and movies I watched. *Of course* we all identify with white protagonists—they're almost always the heroes, the ones with

---

* Sessions is also a vehement opponent of affirmative action, which strikes me as powerful irony: the reality we live in is, by default, a robust affirmative action program for white men.

the power to change things, to affect things rather than simply *be affected*.

As James Baldwin put it,

> You go to white movies and, like everybody else, you fall in love with Joan Crawford, and you root for the Good Guys who are killing off the Indians. It comes as a great psychological collision when you realize all of these things are really metaphors for your oppression, and will lead into a kind of psychological warfare in which you may perish.[24]

And whether it be because you are female, brown, queer, or in any other way visibly *other* from white, able-bodied, cisgender, heterosexual men, it feels like a kind of violence when you suddenly have to reckon with the differences of the body you're in. Not because of some innate qualities embedded in those differences, but because of all the assumptions made about the body you're in that you have to confront.

Coming of age in particular constitutes a jarring emergence of double-consciousness—of being forced to see yourself through the eyes of others even as you're still trying to form a sense of self.

During a summer trip to Florida to visit relatives, my aunt, poolside, remarked upon my fourteen-year-old form in a bathing suit: *When did you get breasts? How big are those things?* I felt ashamed—and not just because my body was suddenly a spectacle. I already knew it was. *How big are those things* was precisely how I felt about the strange lumps of flesh that had sprouted from my body. They were separate from me.

While I was deeply embarrassed by my aunt's commentary,

there was an element of identification, of relating to her perspective. It seemed more of a farce to me that people could look at me and assume that this newly hatched female form was somehow *me* instead of something that *had happened to* me.

And yet, that is the presumption: that the general shape you come to take imbues you with certain "female" traits—to be accommodating, empathetic, emotional, sexual (but not too sexual!). Our bodies become shorthand for a grab-bag of assumptions, some of which we grow into, some of which we bristle against.

My femaleness has always been something that seemed to fit me poorly—at turns an oversized garment I could not fill, or some skimpy rag out of which I spilled.

I've already made a mistake by calling the femaleness "mine." It's never felt like a thing I owned so much as a general shape I grew into that seemed to offer me up for public consumption.

The phrase "gender is a construct" might strike some as academic claptrap, but ask any woman how they were treated before and after puberty, and you're well on your way to understanding not just the truth, but how fucked up that truth is—the extent to which the entire world, and the way you must navigate it, is irrevocably changed.

Also at fourteen, I remember walking down the street with K. and H., my closest friends, in the North Carolina college town where I grew up. We flinched when three men started catcalling us. *Yeah, baby. Look at that ass.* I remember feeling bewildered and disarmed. Having a reputation as being the outspoken one, I felt vaguely responsible for doing something about it. But I did nothing.

One of the most humiliating aspects of that moment was that in doing nothing, it felt like I had *allowed them* to do something to us. This is one of the most nefarious aspects of predatory behavior: it makes the target of the behavior feel complicit. You might be going about your business, and then someone who has more power than you demands engagement—the kind in which even your refusal does not always free you, forcing you to play a part in a scene you had no interest in even auditioning for.

A couple hours after the encounter with those men, my friends and I piled back into the car and started our drive home. That's when I spotted the men, still roving the sidewalk not far from where we'd encountered them. *Wait!* I told H., who was driving. *Slow down.* I rolled down the window, started shouting at them the very same things they had lobbed at us: *Yeah, baby. Look at that ass.* It was a humbling and educational moment because, of course, they loved it. I was startled in my naïveté: I had turned the tables, but the tables had not turned.

I didn't have the language for it then, but this was one of the first times I experienced how my words would always be shaped by my appearance—how they would be heard differently. How they would often weigh less. How the expectations of my femaleness would become a thing I would repeatedly have to explain, justify, respond to, contradict.

The same was true of my brownness. Growing up in the South, I quickly learned how to translate the questions "What are you?" and "Where are you from?" Obviously, "human" and "North Carolina by way of Connecticut and California" didn't cut it. What they wanted was for me to explain the parts of me that *weren't white.* I came to accept the question, and as I got older, played around with responses. Sometimes I'd say I was "half white" (and in response to "What's the other half?" I'd add "half non-white"). Sometimes I'd say I was "mostly human." I played dumb, and answered as literally as possible in an attempt to force people to examine what they were saying, what they actually wanted to know, and whether it was a reasonable thing to ask of a virtual stranger.

This was hardly unique to my experience of growing up in the South. When I was in my twenties, I spoke to a literary agent in New York about a collection of short stories I had written. She was excited by my writing, but concerned that there wasn't enough of an "overarching emotional arc or theme" to connect the stories. "For instance," she wrote,

> Jhumpa Lahiri's short stories have something larger to say about first generation Indian-Americans—about marriage, family dynamics, adjusting to a new country, etc., and I'm not quite sure what you're trying to say here . . . I'd like to see more of your background woven into the stories.

Better yet, one of the stories in the collection I had shared with her included a protagonist who was an Indian writer in conversation with her agent:

> "Nobody biting yet," the agent writes, suggesting that I start something new—something that "takes advantage of your heritage. . . . How about a novel with an Indian-in-America theme? Sort of Jhumpa Lahiri-ish?"

It was darkly comical that the real-life agent was echoing the fictional situation I had written. At the time, I took her feedback to heart. Yet I found myself wondering about what she meant by my "background." My primary identity is not as a first-generation Indian-American. I identify more as an ambiguously brown American—one who decided to learn Spanish in part because so many people assume I'm Latina, that I figured I should be able to at least say, "No soy Latina. Mi padre es de India y mi madre es blanca—de Estados Unidos." The unifying theme in the stories I gave the agent was precisely this: my characters were shape-shifters whose appearances were often in tension with their self-identification.

I abandoned those stories, and it wasn't until almost a decade after my conversation with that agent that I thought: Would she ever have said "I'd like to see more of your background woven into the stories" to a white male writer?

When you ask what terrain a white male fiction writer might explore, the sky is generally the limit. (In fact, it's rare to even see that question posed.) But if you're queer, brown, female, differently abled, etc., it's expected that you'll discuss *that*. More than discuss it, you're often tasked with explaining it—what happened, why you look the way you do, why you identify the way you do in contrast to the expectations projected on you based on your appearance. The conversation you're supposed to have is the conversation white folks would like to have based on what they see. They're the kinds of questions we almost never think to ask white folks themselves—particularly white men.

As an "other," the complex human you are ends up being reduced to a handful of visible traits. It's a kind of censorship: the world's questions shape how you define yourself, how you explain yourself. Even individuals and organizations with good intentions end up reinforcing this heavily policed line: there are a number of scholarship and funding initiatives for marginalized individuals, but to be eligible or to have a real chance of being selected, you usually have to prove that this identity is core to who you are and the work you do.

To move beyond the perceived notions of your identity can be destabilizing for other people. As a teenager, I recall a drunken frat boy who, after seeing me teaching a friend basic dance steps, ambled over to ask what kind of dancing we were doing. I told him it was salsa. His brow furrowed. Then he asked, "What are you?" I translated his question, replied that I was half Indian. I watched his face travel a journey of utter bewilderment. There were about eight long seconds of silence before he came out with: "Then . . . shouldn't you be Indian dancing?" Despite the offensiveness of the question, I laugh when I think about it. In the moment, I recall telling him that I knew he had had a lot to drink, but that I wanted him to try to remember the conversation when he woke up the next morning, and to think about what he'd assumed and why it was problematic. He nodded, a little confused, the effort of earnestly trying to follow my instructions written on his face.

I sometimes get nostalgic about the transparent way that boy responded to me. I knew exactly where he stood. He felt like less of a threat than so many of the folks who count themselves as allies while their bigotry goes unexamined, closeted behind a veneer of progressive cred or good intentions. This outright confusion or even straightforward bigotry and sexism can be easier to navigate than the more veiled way so many Americans—particularly those on the Left—deal with their confusion about, and fear of, otherness.

FLAWED OBJECTIVITY ON THE LEFT

IN THE DAYS AND WEEKS AFTER the election, as shock gave way to analysis and discussion of practical next steps, there was a common refrain: *We must reach across the aisle. We must find common ground. We must leave our differences behind.* It was that kind of sentiment that was behind some of the tense conversations that emerged when the Women's March on Washington was initially being organized. When black participants and organizers engaged in online conversation—about intersectionality, recognizing privilege, listening more and talking less—some white women took offense.

As one fifty-year-old white woman told a *New York Times* reporter after cancelling her and her daughters' plans to attend the march: "This is a women's march . . . We're supposed to be allies in equal pay, marriage, adoption. Why is it now about, 'White women don't understand black women'?"[25]

Broad calls to come together as allies sound reasonable enough. Who argues against solidarity, after all? Except this kind of broad appeal often serves as shorthand for a more nefarious policing, the subtext of which is this: unless the particular concerns or injustices you face are shared by the most privileged among us, they aren't worthwhile, or they're a distraction from some other more "important" issue.

It's a sentiment that seems to surface any time we're in a politically charged moment. Just ten days after the election, Columbia professor Mark Lilla published an op-ed in *The New York Times* titled "The End of Identity Liberalism." At first, Lilla makes a quick nod to the importance of diversity to establish his liberal cred: "It is a truism that America has become a more diverse country. It is also a beautiful thing to watch." But he struggles to locate any substantive value in this fact beyond the aesthetics, arguing that diversity should not "shape our politics" because it is "disastrous as a foundation for democratic politics in our ideological age."

Lilla is concerned with acknowledging differences because of their potential to alienate the "average voter":

How to explain to the average voter the supposed moral urgency of giving college students the right to choose the designated gender pronouns to be used when addressing them? How not to laugh along with those voters at the story of a University of Michigan prankster who wrote in "His Majesty"?[26]

Here we see Lilla—like Jake Tapper trying to defend the inane questions ABC chose to ask presidential candidates in 2008—cynically using "the average voter" as a beard for his own argument that gender identity is a petty issue. For a professor of history, Lilla seems staggeringly unaware of how his arguments echo those of earlier generations' bigotry—finding it laughable that marginalized Americans be afforded a right as basic as being recognized.

As is usually the case with those who argue that we need to stop being complex individuals in order to appeal to a broader swath of Americans, Lilla never explicitly states what this "average voter" looks like. In the absence of that, we're left to fill in the blanks. Presumably these average voters are white men like Mark Lilla who think that one's identity and one's politics can somehow be separated, that our skin color or gender identity can be stripped away like a costume—not unlike the conceit of that white, male British subject in Boorde's guide.

Calls like Lilla's that hinge on appealing to the "average voter" or "average American" urgently need to be unpacked. Given that only roughly 30 percent of Americans are white men—which doesn't parse what percentage of them identify as transgender or queer—that leaves a minimum of 70 percent of Americans whose identities and perceived identities directly impact their safety, health, and income in this country. The "average American" and "average voter" is not some monolithic contingent, despite its common usage as shorthand for "white American." There's a similar principle at work in the way the phrase "working-class American" tends to serve as shorthand for "white, working-class American," despite the fact that the majority of the American working class is part of an ethnic or racial minority.[27] The erasure in terms like this makes calls to reach across the aisle and appeal to the "forgotten American working class" deeply problematic. Organizing and finding common cause across racial and ethnic lines to organize as working-class Americans is necessary and pragmatic. But to reach across the aisle to specifically address working-class Americans based on their whiteness is to pander to the same kind of racial divides that Trump exploited to garner votes.

The subtextual conclusion for folks like Lilla is that bringing racial, gender, and sexual identity into the arena of politics prevents liberalism "from becoming a unifying force capable of governing."[28] This is its own fundamentalist ideology presented in the Trojan horse of "neutrality" and inclusivity. It's also an odd argument—while ostensibly made in the interests of not alienating these unspecified "other Americans," it tidily alienates any American who finds their non-white identity relevant to their politics.

After the election, Bernie Sanders told a Boston crowd, "It's not good enough for somebody to say, 'Hey, I'm a Latina, vote for me.' That is not good enough. I have to know whether that Latina is going to stand up with the working class of this country and is going to take on big money interests."[29] It was an instance in which the statement was so obvious, it made it difficult to understand the purpose of mentioning it. Given that we live in a country where fewer than one in five members of Congress are women or minorities, and given that one of the most qualified people ever to run for the office of president was a woman who *did not win*, it's evident that women and minorities need to do *far more* than simply show up to win office.[30] His statement reflects a problematic implication that women and minorities are "playing" the race or gender "card." It's true that it's going to take more than asserting our brownness or queerness or femaleness to rally Americans. But it's also true that our experience navigating our lives with these identities does allow us insight and perspective into the problems that most need to be addressed. Speaking from these specific experiences can enable us to make powerful common cause with all Americans who seek a more egalitarian country and better quality of life.

The ahistoric sensibility that Lilla expresses (and Sanders alluded to) is at the heart of the "All Lives Matter" response to the Black Lives Matter movement. If you're ignorant of history and of the continuing institutional racism that defines our current reality—black Americans incarcerated at a rate five times that of white Americans; black Americans twice as likely to be living in poverty—then the message that "black lives matter" becomes at best meaningless, and at worst a provocation, as though black lives matter more than white lives.[31] This fundamental mis-understanding of the framework of Black Lives Matter is similar to how many approach feminism. Instead of recognizing it as a straightforward response to an imbalance in need of correction, the fight for equality is disparaged or misunderstood as some sort of extremist political stance. At the heart of it is this notion that rights are somehow a zero-sum game.

Granted, there are some who are vehemently opposed to the BLM movement because they are old-fashioned racists who find the mere existence of black Americans a provocation. But there are plenty of Americans—particularly those who might describe themselves as "apolitical" (or, god forbid, "color-blind")—who fall into this same trap, tacitly joining a racist or misogynistic camp simply by denying the reality of the bigoted America we currently live in. It's a kind of destructive glass-half-full-ism in which the willfulness to live in a "post-racist" or egalitarian society blinds these Americans to the reality of the world—a reality in which their work to balance the scales is desperately needed.

In a country where one's quality of life—and even life expectancy—is directly impacted by their skin color, sexual orientation, gender, or gender identity, the reality is that claiming you aren't "political" constitutes its own fundamentalist political stance. If we do not recognize the reality of inequality, we perpetuate it.

Toward the end of his op-ed, Lilla issues a warning that "Liberals should bear in mind that the first identity movement in American politics was the Ku Klux Klan, which still exists. Those who play the identity game should be prepared to lose it." And here's the crux: those who support this ahistoric and privileged line of thinking see identity as a game one plays, because they cannot help but think of themselves as the default, as the vantage point of a more universal and objective perspective, of whiteness as the absence of complexity and identity. Other identities are deemed handicaps, hindering our ability to see neutrally or inclusively. Instead of being valued as vital and intrinsic aspects of our selves, our identities are treated as superfluous layers that we might simply remove like a sweater in a too-warm room.

It's the same sensibility that is at the core of Jeff Sessions's worldview. When the news broke that the FBI had been compiling a report on "black identity extremist" groups that constitute a possible terrorist threat—clearly a reference to the nonviolent group Black Lives Matter—Sessions revealed his commitment to his biases: "I am aware that there are groups that do have an extraordinary commitment to their racial identity," he said. "Some have transformed themselves even into violent activists."[32] When representative Karen Bass of California then asked him, "Are you aware of white organizations that do this as well? Given that white supremacy is a well-documented, well-researched movement, such as the neo-Nazis, the Ku Klux Klan, etc.—are they white identity extremists?," Sessions seemed suddenly confused, asking her to repeat the question. Bass says, "Is there a term or a report on white identity extremists? You mentioned you were familiar with black people who identify with their racial identity." Sessions responds, "Yes, but it's not coming to me at this moment."[33]

Whether from deliberateness or ignorance, Sessions stumbles over the prospect of white supremacists as terrorists.

In his op-ed, Lilla concluded with a call for "a post-identity liberalism, and it should draw from the past successes of pre-identity liberalism. Such a liberalism would concentrate on widening its base by appealing to Americans as Americans and emphasizing the issues that affect a vast majority of them."

Americans as Americans. Lilla ends up parroting Sessions.

Yet, as we've seen, the issues that affect the vast majority of Americans are precisely those that affect marginalized Americans.

This kind of entreaty—particularly problematic when it comes from those who purport to be our allies—is exactly what propagates the thinking that our political selves must be these strange laundered identities separate from the needs, fears, and hopes that shape our personal lives. This ideological approach fuels the dissociation most of us experience from our political system. If we don't think of it as a realm in which we can address our true concerns and needs, it's that much easier to dismiss it as a cynical game, a horserace to be played or rigged.

I ONCE GOT INTO an argument with a self-described atheist progressive at a dinner I was hosting. She maintained that religion had been used throughout history as a justification for unspeakable violence and bigotry. I agreed with her on that count. But she moved to the conclusion that those who believe in God simply lack intelligence. I asked her whether she found any discomfort in how her judgment—that all those who believe in God need to be saved from their own ignorance—made her odd bedfellows with the very fundamentalists she was railing against. She didn't. "Nothing good has come from religion," she insisted.

But what about the civil rights movement, someone at the table suggested. *What about Martin Luther King, Jr.?*

"He could have done it without religion," she said. And that was the moment when I stopped trying to point out how absurd her supposition was, because I felt she had done that work for me.

This belief system shares much with Lilla's: that the individual lenses through which we see the world can be stripped away, leaving some more universal, objective perspective. In order to sustain this belief, you have to—literally—whitewash history and reality.

These aren't just abstract concepts. Whitewashing reality—being blind to the white, male subjectivity that often stands in for objectivity—has concrete repercussions. Consider this: women are twice as likely as men to develop post-traumatic stress disorder (PTSD)—not surprising when you consider that one in six women are survivors of rape or attempted rape.[34] Yet most of the foundational medical studies on PTSD and PTSD treatment have focused on male veterans of war.[35]

Despite many medications having different effects on women than on men, women make up only one-third of the participants in medical and drug studies.[36] The fallout is documentable: a 2001 study from the Government Accountability Office found that eight out of ten drugs that were pulled from the market for having serious adverse health effects posed much more severe risks for women.[37]

The erasures and oversights built into our default biased objectivity are also self-fulfilling: In 2005, Larry Summers—

president of Harvard University at the time—publicly stated that one of the reasons there weren't as many female scientists at elite universities may be due to "innate" differences between men and women. Writer Rebecca Solnit reminds us that while he was president of Harvard, the number of tenured jobs offered to women fell from 36 to 13 percent.[38]

It's a reminder of the real-world impact of skewed or unseen narratives, and a reminder, too, of blindness and erasure that pervades even those realms we like to think of as being apolitical, like science. There is no "apolitical" or "objective realm. Being a scientist does not strip someone of the susceptibility to deeply rooted biases and blind spots. Good science is as much about asking the right questions as seeking answers. The best science often asks questions of *those answers,* moving our knowledge forward by recognizing that no answer is ever complete or final. It is always ever a reflection of the limits of our knowledge at the time, which demands a certain humility of us all.

THE STRENGTH IN SUBJECTIVITIES

O N AUGUST 9, 2014, A white policeman in Ferguson, Missouri, shot and killed Michael Brown—an unarmed black teenager. Given the reality we live in, where a quarter of the people whom police kill are black males even though they make up only 6 percent of the population, Brown's death was far from guaranteed to make headlines.[39]

The sustained protests in Ferguson started with a memorial of flowers and candles on the street where Brown's blood still stained the pavement. The next day, more and more men, women, and children gathered in the street. In response, Ferguson and St. Louis police came out in full force, dressed in riot gear with shields and face masks. The fact that the protest was able to have such a notable impact—solidifying the Black Lives Matter movement and forcing a nationwide reckoning with police violence against the black community—was a result not only of persistent protesters but of coordination among a variety of progressive movements and leaders. Working in tandem, organizers from different movements were able to take what could have been a short-lived uprising that ended in arrests and police violence, and ensure it would have staying power.

Support came from across the country: white and black activists with experience in direct action; activist street medics from Chicago who helped protesters contend with rubber-bullet wounds and tear gas.

The mobilization in Ferguson reminded writer and organizer L.A. Kauffman of an earlier moment in history:

> [A]t Mayday 1971 . . . veterans of the black civil rights movement organized their caravan to bring food and other supplies to the thousands of mostly white protesters who had been arrested after trying to shut down the federal government in protest of the Vietnam War. Then, as in Ferguson, the gestures of support had a political resonance beyond the concrete assistance being offered, highlighting the longer, deeper influences that carried over from one movement to the next.[40]

This kind of cross-cultural and cross-issue solidarity can also be seen in the Standing Rock protests from early 2016 through early 2017. Some two thousand US military veterans, organized by former Marine and Baltimore police officer Michael Wood, Jr., arrived to support the indigenous American–led action to stop an oil pipeline from being constructed near the Standing Rock Indian Reservation. Protesters described their mission as "serving as a kind of 'human shield' between peaceful demonstrators and police"[41]—standing up to the tear gas, rubber bullets, and sound cannons that were regularly being used against peaceful protesters. Veterans recognized the privilege that they had, and the message it would send Americans to see men and women who have defended our country visibly opposing what Trump has called a project that "serve[s] the national interest."[42] Their presence challenged this narrative.

Veterans also participated in "forgiveness ceremonies" while at Standing Rock. As writer Naomi Klein recounts, "For hours, hundreds of vets lined up to beg forgiveness of the elders for crimes committed against Indigenous peoples over centuries by the military institutions they served."[43] It's another reminder that, even when protests "fail" at their stated objectives, there are other successes and moments of profound healing—ones we may scarcely be able to envision at the time—that come out of collective actions.

We're seeing more and more of this kind of solidarity and intersectionality in protests. In the wake of Occupy Wall Street, Black Lives Matter, immigrant rights, and climate justice movements have all been gaining power and visibility. And while a number of them are focused around specific identities or objectives, this has not stopped them from collaborating and organizing together. Indeed, that collaboration has added to their strength. It makes calls to "move past" identity politics or "reach across the aisle" sound not only tone-deaf, but strategically counterproductive.

History shows that some of the greatest democratic achievements that brought Americans together—and benefited all of them—have come out of movements that hinged on identity.

Consider the civil rights movement making huge strides toward equality, or ACT UP's advocacy and protests which led to better treatment and medication options for those with HIV/AIDS, thereby helping to save millions of lives.

Where people like Lilla see narrowness and fragmentation, history reveals multiplicity and strength. ACT UP, a movement predominately composed of gay men, gained clout through direct-action trainings that were led by women who had cut their teeth in the feminist wave of the 1970s.[44] As Kauffman reminds us, it's the marginalized people in this country who are responsible for the bulk of social change: "When you actually look on the ground at who is organizing, carrying the work, shaping the visions, taking the risks, it's disproportionately women—often queer women of color."[45]

There are countless examples of women like this who are the architects of social change, but whose contributions go unnoticed or have been erased from most history books. Take Pauli Murray, first in her class at Howard University's law school back in the 1940s, and the only woman enrolled. One of her law school papers argued that segregation violated the Thirteenth and Fourteenth Amendments of the Constitution—an argument that her professor would use to help win *Brown v. Board of Education*. She also went on to publish a law review article that was used by Ruth Bader Ginsburg to successfully argue that the Equal Protection Clause applied to women. There are many alsos in the life of Murray: In 1965, she also suggested to feminist Betty Friedan that they organize an NAACP for women. So she, Friedan, and a group of other women launched the National Organization for Women—now the largest organization of feminist activists in the United States—the following year. Murray was also queer—a fact that she did not discuss openly. She was frustrated by societal pressures to divvy up her identities into tidy boxes, writing that she hated "to be fragmented into Negro at one time, woman at another, or worker at another."[46] The full force of her power and perspective—as is the case with all of us—lies in the confluence of these identities.

RECOGNIZING THE CENTRALITY OF those who have been historically marginalized requires unearthing the histories that live outside of the more conventionally edited—and sometimes explicitly censored—narratives that populate our textbooks and popular consciousness. And it requires, too, taking a step back from this bizarrely pervasive narrative that the most inclusive "identity" is one that strips away any quality that veers from white heteronormative maleness—a stifling category that even most white heteronormative men fail to find enough oxygen in.

We need to return to the lessons of an era when the "the personal is the political" was more than a slogan on faded and peeling bumper stickers. The concept came out of the second wave of feminism in the late 1960s. But it was the black queer feminist organization the Combahee River Collective that tapped its broader implications, articulating the true stakes and potential of the principle. In their 1977 statement they wrote, "[W]e are dealing with the implications of race and class as well as sex":

> We believe that the most profound and potentially
> the most radical politics come directly out of our own
> identity. We are actively committed to struggling against
> racial, sexual, heterosexual, and class oppression and
> see as our particular task the development of integrated
> analysis and practice based on the fact that the major

systems of oppression are interlocking. The synthesis of these oppressions creates the conditions of our lives.[47]

Their conclusion bridges that gap between the personal and political in a way that comes to the opposite conclusion of those who insist that appealing to the default white male perspective is the most politically effective approach. "If Black women were free," they write, "it would mean that everyone else would have to be free since our freedom would necessitate the destruction of all the systems of oppression."

Audre Lorde, too, famously encouraged us to refuse to accept the narrative that our differences are a problem or challenge:

> As women, we have been taught to either ignore our differences, or to view them as causes for separation and suspicion rather than forces for change. Without community there is no liberation, only the most vulnerable and temporary armistice between an individual and her oppression. But community must not mean a shedding of our differences, nor the pathetic pretense that these differences do not exist.
>
> Those of us who stand outside the circle of this society's definition of acceptable women; those of us who have been forged in the crucible of difference—those of us who are poor, who are lesbians, who are Black, who are older—know that survival is not an academic skill. It is learning how to take our differences and make them strengths. For the master's tools will never dismantle the master's house. They may allow us temporarily to beat him at his own game, but they will never enable us to bring about genuine change.[48]

These arguments are not *contrary* to broad political appeals for Americans to unite and come together around issues such as class and the economy. Rather, they're reminders that what unites so many of us are the specific ways in which class and economy impact us *because of* our marginalized status.

What if the much maligned "identity politics" were not by default viewed as divisive? What if, instead, we looked to identity politics as a rich resource, one that contains the seeds of a powerful vision for true economic and social justice?

IT IS THE MARGINALIZED among us who can most accurately testify to that distance between American promises—of equality, life, liberty, and the pursuit of happiness—and American reality.

Giving a shit about the personal experiences of marginalized Americans is not something the Left simply needs to pay lip service to in the interests of being politically correct. Nor is it something we should give ourselves a pat on the back for paying attention to. It is at the very core of our ability to envision a reality in which true egalitarianism exists, and it is the most direct and effective way to build that reality.

The arguments from Lorde and the Combahee River Collective are based on concrete lessons from history. When the perspectives and concerns of those who experience the most discrimination are front and center in our movements, we all win freer lives—lives in which we are able to inhabit the full scope of our identities without fear that straying from expected norms will disqualify us from core rights and privileges.

I've often found myself in conversation with white allies who have a hard time understanding what their role might be in this movement, aside from the important work of recognizing their privilege. But part of recognizing privilege is also examining how walking the path of privilege may have hemmed in other aspects of their identities, or otherwise encouraged them to perform an identity that limits their sense of self.

Beyond that, white allies also have a major role to play in making and holding the space for the narratives of those who have been historically marginalized. That may look like listening more than speaking, or even more actively creating space for marginalized people by noticing and addressing situations when they aren't in the room. It may look like standing on the frontlines of protests since marginalized people face higher risks of police violence. It may look like white people calling other white people out for perpetuating bigotry—whether blatant or subtle. But above all, it means recognizing that race, gender, and sexual orientation are not "issues" to be addressed as separate from a broader political movement.

It makes intuitive sense that the most marginalized among us are often the ones who are most committed to taking action: our very lives and livelihood are under attack in a way that can make day-to-day reality at best a challenge and at worst unsurvivable. In many respects, marginalized Americans live in a separate country from white male Americans, with separate likelihoods for survival and success. Black men in America live, on average, five years fewer than white American men.[49] One in three black men will go to prison in their lifetime. Black women are three times more likely than white women to be incarcerated. Black Americans receive sentences that are 10 percent longer than white Americans convicted of the same crimes.[50] One in four transgender Americans will be physically assaulted for the simple fact that they are transgender.[51] The wage gap in our country translates into women losing out on over $400,000 over the lifetime of their careers. For women of color, that number doubles.[52] It's a troubling reality—one that is generally ignored, given short shrift, or outright denied.

Since the outset of Trump's presidency, there has been a renewed panic around what it means for facts and reality to come under attack or be ignored. Trump peddled fear to Americans during his campaign—citing a "crime wave" in our country despite the fact that violent crime is at a historic low.[53] He repeatedly stated that Russia did not interfere with the 2016 elections, despite findings from US intelligence agencies that it did.[54] A PolitiFact study showed that 70 percent of Trump's statements during the campaign were false. In his first 298 days in office, he made more than 1,600 false or misleading claims—roughly six per day.[55]

Two months into Trump's presidency, psychoanalyst Joel Whitebook published an op-ed in *The New York Times* arguing that Trump's strategic methods constitute an attack on our relation to reality. "The fear here," he writes, "is that if the 45th president can maintain this manic pace, he may wear down the resistance and Trump-exhaustion will set in, causing the disoriented experience of reality he has created to grow ever stronger and more insidious."[56]

It's a reasonable fear, yet it's one that the majority of Americans—the black, brown, female, and queer majority among us—have been navigating for centuries. If we're looking for tips on how to survive such an onslaught on reality, there are no better experts than marginalized Americans. Which is why we need to make a concerted effort to shift these concerns from the margin to the center.

Marginalized Americans are the *heart* of the movement. And they always have been.

TURNING THE TABLES

THERE'S POWER TO UNEARTHING AND recognizing the centrality of the narratives of marginalized Americans— especially in a political moment where we're facing a resurgence of misogyny and racism under the banner of euphemized language like "locker room talk" and the "alt-right." Parallel to this resurgence, we're seeing a remarkable pushback—a reclaiming of narratives.

On October 5, 2017, *The New York Times* broke the story that influential Hollywood producer Harvey Weinstein had paid off multiple women who accused him of sexual harassment.[57] After the initial article, dozens of women came forward to accuse Weinstein of sexual harassment and assault. Weinstein was consequently fired from his company's board.[58] Then came accusations that actor Kevin Spacey had groped or assaulted numerous teenage boys and young men. The TV series that Spacey starred in was canceled.[59] Next, the story broke that comedian Louis C.K. masturbated in front of five women. His movie and upcoming comedy special were nixed.[60] Then came accusations that Alabama Republican candidate for Senate Roy Moore had sexually assaulted multiple minors. He lost the election.[61]

The bottle had come uncorked, and women's voices rang out. As more and more allegations against men surfaced, the hashtag #metoo went viral, with women across the country posting their personal stories of sexual violence and harassment to Facebook and Twitter.

During this same stretch of time, an old colleague reached out to me. She wanted to see if I was interested in coming forward about our former boss—the one who had responded to my request for a raise by asking me if I needed help paying my rent. The fact was, I didn't have anything too damning to say about him apart from the fact that he always struck me as a creep—someone I tried to avoid interacting with whenever possible. When I didn't get the raise I asked for—refusing to accept his terms—I was able to negotiate a better title instead. A few months later, when I received a better-paying job elsewhere, I gave notice. My boss was furious, railing against my so-called betrayal. It was gross and unprofessional, but I'd end up feeling relieved at how tame this behavior would come to seem. After #metoo, about a dozen former colleagues of ours from that publication came together and shared our stories about our abusive former boss. It was so much worse than I had known at the time. What I learned: He had shown a photo of his penis to one colleague, had made a habit of taking photos of another while she worked, had sent explicitly sexual emails, had carried on an emotionally and sexually abusive affair with a woman some thirty years his junior . . . the list went on. While a few of us had even been friends when we worked together, it became clear that we had not thought to share so many of our stories—of being harassed, abused, or mistreated—with each other at the time. Together, we realized how we had each worked to minimize the abuse.

These kinds of stories are shocking but not surprising. After the election, M.—who told me her story about being sexually assaulted while traveling—was not my only friend who was re-examining sexual transgressions from her past. Our sense of powerlessness as we saw Trump rise to power did not simply leave us quiet and chastened. It was no coincidence the dominoes began to fall—allegation after allegation against men in powerful positions—all within the first year of Trump's presidency. The rise of Donald Trump forced a new lens on our stories.

M. and I and every other woman I know, and every other woman that you know, have had conversations about the kinds of episodes that surfaced during the outpouring of #metoo testimony. Conversations where we speak haltingly of experiences with men—experiences that have lodged themselves like gristle in our teeth or even more deeply in our bones. In safe spaces, we hold them up to the light, not necessarily with hope that we will gain some understanding of why they happened, but simply to try to own them in a way that intercedes so that they cannot own us. To allow oxygen in the room. To dispel the shame that seems to always trail behind them.

Consider:

S.'s voice so small, I pressed the phone to my ear until it hurt.

"Last night . . ." she started. Then stopped. Then started again. "I mean, I said 'no,' but maybe I didn't say it clearly. Or enough."

J. walking with me up Ninth Avenue, speaking in a breathless rush—an attempted tone of matter-of-factness: "There were things that I did . . . that I let people do to me . . . that I did not want to do but felt I was supposed to."

A lurching toward locating the control and agency in the situation. *What I should have done is x or y.* Or: *I chose to, even if later, I came to regret it.* An attempt to find a narrative to house the experience. To contain it so that it will not leak and get onto other things.

The experience may come and go, but there is always some residue left behind. We can tell the story of what happened, but we cannot control how those stories are heard and understood.

This is part of why it often takes so long for allegations against people like Harvey Weinstein, Louis C.K., and Roy Moore to go public. Rumors abound—how many times have I been warned to be careful around certain men I've worked with?—but the risk of coming forward has hardly seemed worth it. It has historically involved being discredited, having your character attacked, your existence flattened into a single narrative that follows you around for the rest of your life: *that woman who accused [name of notable man] of [name of crime].* We live in a society where an estimated 90 percent of rapes go unreported. Of those that are reported, the perpetrators are rarely brought to justice. Which is another way of saying that the meaning of our stories—stories of our bodies and what happens to them when we take them out into the world—are always being revised, rewritten, erased.

This emergent reality, in which we're acknowledging that it's unreasonable and intolerable for these kinds of abuses to occur every day, is incredibly heartening. We're seeing a substantive shift of the shame and blame from ourselves to the rightful owners of it.

We have an opportunity now to not only find agency and hold onto power by resurfacing or revising our narratives; if we can testify to the full impact these experiences have on our lives, we can collectively shift the narrative, forcing these aggressors—or at least the culture around them—to reckon with their responsibility and culpability. Part of the work is making the impact and costs of this behavior more visible.

Where once stories were framed so that our experiences were narrated as *what happened to [name of notable man]*, the stories have begun to focus on us, on the repercussions for our lives and our careers, on the fallout of having endured such dehumanizing behavior. The three female journalists who broke the Louis C.K. story for *The New York Times* made this fallout a central part of the story. They included details about how the women are still struggling with the shame and trauma years later, how some of them had to pass up career opportunities in order to avoid further encounters with their abusers and apologists. One woman noted that she accepted an apology from Louis C.K. and that she forgave him, "but the original interaction left her deeply dispirited . . . and was one of the things that discouraged her from pursuing comedy."[62]

These are the kinds of stories that are often the most challenging to tell: what we *didn't* or *couldn't* do as a result of this kind of violence and abuse of power. And that's what makes it all the more necessary and important for them to be heard.

IT WAS ONLY OVER a decade after leaving my former job that I—and many of my and other former colleagues—realized how systemic the abuse was. Our boss usually hired young women who were just starting out in their careers. We were all eager to prove ourselves, and therefore eager to minimize anything that might jeopardize our opportunity to succeed. We internalized the abuse, let it remain a personal problem. It took us years to collectively recognize that this was an issue that could be addressed. A handful of our group went public—with our stories appearing on BuzzFeed and This American Life. Our former boss resigned. It was a kind of power, a kind of consequence, I had never entertained as a real possibility.

The trick now is to not stop with surfacing these individual narratives that focus on individual incidents and men, but to also address the larger social problems that make it possible for this behavior to be so widespread. We need to hit on a narrative that doesn't just respond to subjugation and victimization but that demands a response.

In a 1965 televised debate with William F. Buckley, James Baldwin took a moment to get to the heart of what makes an aggressor. Referencing Alabama sheriff Jim Clark, an official who was notoriously brutal in his crackdown on civil rights protesters, he says, "Something awful must have happened to a human being to be able to put a cattle prod against a woman's breasts . . ."[63] Baldwin turns the tables, questioning the anemia of Clark's humanity to so boldly violate someone else's. The burden of shame is shifted to the rightful owner.

Necessary to turning the tables is the ability to cultivate a healthy sense of outrage—not the kind that burns so fast and bright that it consumes us in the process. We need the kind of vital, slow-burning outrage that keeps us warm, alive, and connected to our vision of the world as *it must be*.

There's something fundamental here that we need to understand more clearly: how these kinds of anecdotes, these revelations of abuse, are not surprising, but the reality they strip bare is still deserving of our outrage. It strikes me that if we wish to not just survive but thrive as human beings, we have to learn how to navigate this line.

Writer Eileen Myles once pondered the issue in terms of female suffering. Responding to a figure of a female Christ that appears in a church in Montreal, she writes:

> Mostly the world can't take it. Because of people's feelings about the delicacy of women and also because of what a meaningless display female suffering simply is. If you belittle us in school, treat us like slaves at home and finally, if you get a woman alone in bed just tell her she's all wrong, no matter what sex you are . . . or maybe just grab one on the street and fuck her real fast—in an alley, or in her own bed.
>
> I mean if that's the way it usually goes for this girl what would be the point in seeing her half nude and nailed up. Where's the contradiction? Could that drive the culture for 2,000 years? No way. Female suffering must be hidden, or nothing can work. It's a man's world and a girl on a cross would be like seeing a dead animal in a trap. We like to eat them, or see them stuffed, we even like to wear them, but watch them suffer? Hear them wail?[64]

Myles beautifully captures the challenge we face. So much of the work we need to do is to move past the cynicism pervading our culture that tells us that our suffering is meaningless: We have to be able to envision a world in which our suffering matters. We have to behave as though it does until the world catches up to the truth of it.

BEFORE AND AFTER MY colleagues and I went public about our abusive former boss, we consistently had to reassure each other—in person and by email—that yes, this is a big deal. Yes, showing employees dick pics, commenting on our appearances, sending emails about sexual positions, trying to give massages, and offering additional work or raises on the condition that it was tied to "helping" us out in a personal way was all unacceptable behavior. It was so easy for us to minimize it, to fall back on our earlier worldview that this kind of behavior is simply part of how the world works. Without the solidarity we established, the ongoing conversations—reminding each other that abusive behavior should not be normal, that the bar needed to be higher—we never would have been able to reclaim our narratives or have the impact we did.

We aren't accustomed to discussing hope as though it were a challenging practice, but it is. And it requires us to examine our complicity in a system that has accepted our status as lesser-than, as subjective where white men have exclusive access to the objective. This work can also be painful. As Baldwin writes of the challenges of both white and black Americans working toward true equality:

> The possibility of liberation which is always real is also
> always painful, since it involves such an overhauling of all
> that gave us our identity . . . We will need every ounce of
> moral stamina we can find. For everything is changing,
> from our notion of politics to our notion of ourselves,
> and we are certain . . . to undergo the torment of being
> forced to surrender far more than we ever realized we had
> accepted.[65]

ON COMPLICITY

WHEN I WAS IN MY early twenties, my white grandmother and I got into a difficult conversation about
my brother. At the time, we didn't know where
he was. In fact, no one had heard from him in months. He had
some mental health issues and, because he was unwilling to see a
therapist, he'd resorted to his own way of handling his situation:
self-medicating with a variety of recreational drugs. My grandmother and I discussed my brother until there was a strange and
sudden lurch in the conversation.

"I just wish it wasn't so hard for you," she said. I was confused by the jump in topic from my brother to what was clearly a reference to both of us. "What do you mean?" I asked. "Just that it's harder for you because you come from a different background," she said. I remember that moment clearly, the sensation of sudden exile from what had initially felt like a space of solidarity and togetherness. It would be one thing if she were responding to something I had said about how I was encountering obstacles in my life because of how I looked and what my background was. But I hadn't. All I'd done was address her concern about my brother.

I've encountered this many times, usually from well-meaning white people—a kind of loose apology that the world is the way it is, which often contains the assumption that any problems or challenges we might have are a result of being "different." It's an oversimplified assertion that can have the effect of pathologizing otherness rather than society's discomfort with that otherness—and in that sense, it's a relative of victim-shaming and -blaming. While I believe this impulse often comes from a place of good intentions, I'm suspicious of what this kind of platitude obscures.

Was my grandmother simply being realistic by pointing out that it is more difficult to be a brown person in this country? Or, was there also some latent acceptance of bigotry—as though it were a kind of natural force at work in the world? It's a way in which being "realistic" or "pragmatic" can look a lot like cynicism. At what point does this convenient crutch (*I hate it, but that's just how it is*) serve as a protective veil for our own latent bigotry and misogyny?

This tricky line between acknowledgment and acceptance isn't just a tough balancing act for white Americans. It's a line that those of us who qualify as "other" must navigate, too. There's The Talk that parents have with their black and brown children, to tell them they should not wear hoodies at night (or, really, ever), should keep their hands visible in stores so that people won't think they're shoplifting, should be aware that just their existence can be deemed a threat to white people and get them killed. There's The Talk parents have with their daughters, to tell them that wearing certain clothing can be deemed by some men to be an invitation for sexual assault, that leaving their drinks unattended could lead to being roofied and raped.

It's a tough line to walk, especially in light of the tendency of marginalized folks to minimize the experiences of our reality—oftentimes in order to try to eke out some sense of control and power. We don't want our lives to be reduced to narratives about how we've been dehumanized.

In a society that has historically insisted that we were "asking for it" or are somehow innately less deserving of respect, opportunity, health, well-being, or simply survival, the standard narratives available to us are insubstantial coping mechanisms: We minimize, we see it from their perspective, we cede the position of protagonist of our own stories in order to accommodate a reality in which we don't have to be the victim. We laugh when we are terrified for our safety. We remain friends with our victimizers without taking them to task. We convince ourselves that this is simply the way the world is. We turn the loathing inward on ourselves.

These are tools for survival, but I wonder, too, how we can navigate and describe the state of the world without tacitly accepting or legitimizing it.

That's just how it is.

It's necessary to recognize and acknowledge the realities of the moment we are in. Yet an equally necessary part of survival is not stopping with adaptation to the world as it is now, but pushing beyond it to lay claim to the world as it should and must be.

There is a vital and necessary strength to our subjectivities. Marginalized people know what it's like to hold multiple realities as we navigate a culture in which our experiences are so frequently minimized or erased. At a time when a growing number of Americans feel their realities are under attack, we have a leg up. Who better to appeal to a broad swath of Americans than people who are schooled not only in the rhetoric of white male subjectivity ("objectivity"), but in a richer perspective and experience? It's a perspective that allows us to speak with honesty, empathy, and compassion to those who feel unseen, those whose experiences do not seem to fit within the rubric of what's expected of them in our society—in other words, nearly everyone.

I bristle against the notion that it is always the brown, queer, and otherwise "others" who have to lead the way in addressing the problems of inequality and bigotry in this country—no real substantive change can come without white people recognizing their privilege and common causes to become allies of movements that seek true equality. But I also recognize the ways I, too, have been complicit in perpetuating these problems and inequalities— by cynically counting myself apart, by neutering my narrative and aspiring to a tone of false objectivity in my writing that is, at its heart, me trying to speak in a voice that is not my own, trying to use the master's tools to dismantle the master's house.

AFTER THE ELECTION, MY friend T. told me her story about watching the Anita Hill/Clarence Thomas hearings. In 1991, Hill testified that Clarence Thomas had sexually harassed her while he was her supervisor at the Department of Education and the Equal Employment Opportunity Commission. She said that Thomas had asked her out repeatedly, and that when she said no, he continually discussed sexual topics with her in the workplace.[66]

Watching the televised hearings, T. told me, gave her a strange sense of vertigo: so much of the behavior that Hill was describing was what she had experienced years back, when she had been working for a man who served as her mentor.

He often made overtures that made her uncomfortable— turning the conversation to sexual topics, glancing at her body. But she still valued his experience and guidance, so she found ways to live with it, minimize it. It never went *too* far, she said. But, still, she was seeing the behavior differently in retrospect. While watching the hearings one day, she got a phone call from that same mentor. She hadn't heard from him in years. He was watching the hearings, too, he said. He wanted to know whether what Thomas did to Hill was what he had done to her.

This was the point at which T. paused her story. She looked at me and shook her head in disbelief. "You know what I did?" she asked. "I told him 'no.' I told him it was fine. I reassured him." I've marched alongside T. at a number of protests. I've seen her defend and advance the rights and voices of teenagers in the foster care and juvenile justice systems. As someone who is fiercely progressive and politically engaged, T. struggled—as so many of us do—to understand how she could minimize her experience in that way.

It's the same kind of minimizing that we saw from United Nations Ambassador Nikki Haley at an April 2017 lunch for UN Security Council ambassadors and their spouses. Trump, sitting beside her, said into the mic: "She's doing a good job. Now does everybody like Nikki? Otherwise she could be easily replaced. Right?" Haley laughed, her smile a kind of desperate rictus. It was the smile so many of us have smiled, the laugh so many of us have laughed.[67]

It's notable that 53 percent of white women voted for Trump—a professed sexual predator.[68] What does it mean that these women either decided his behavior was reasonable, or that they somehow thought that this "personal" aspect of his life was separate from his politics?

Gloria Steinem, in her memoir *My Life on the Road*, writes about how she tried to dissociate herself from her mother when she was younger—because she saw her mother as passive, meek, having struggled with mental illness and given up a career as a journalist to raise a family. It was a stance she came to revise when she discovered "that we were alike in many ways—something I either hadn't seen or couldn't admit out of fear that I would share her fate."[69] It's a denial so many of us can relate to. We want to believe we aren't subject to the same forces that limit others' lives. We want to feel we're free to be and do anything we choose. Sometimes we become so attached to this heady narrative, that we'll throw our true allies—and even ourselves—under the bus.

There's a related psychological term for it: "system justification theory," whereby people rationalize existing social, economic, or political realities. It's the everyday American equivalent of journalism's "status quo" bias. We want so desperately to believe that we're inhabiting an even playing field that we deny the unpleasant reality we actually inhabit. Writer and activist Eric Liu cites a number of studies that bear this out. One of them, conducted at Stanford, concluded that "The more participants reported feeling powerless, the more they believed that economic inequality was fair and legitimate."[70]

It's frighteningly easy for so many of us in this country to empathize with those who abuse their power. After all, we all grow up to be straight white men until we're forced to recognize that we aren't. It's a tension evident in the fact that *Time*'s 2017 Person of the Year was the The Silence Breakers—all the women who had come forward about being sexually assaulted or harassed. The runner-up for the honor? President Trump.[71] What better evidence of how we're wrestling with what power means and where it resides. The question now is how we choose to access power—through emulation of those who wield it by force or fiat, or through collectivity and solidarity?

A part of our basic survival is understanding the motivations of those who exercise power over us. A black boy in America has to confront the stereotype of being prone to criminality—as the owner of a store follows him around, he's conscious of keeping his hands visible; he's had The Talk. In this context, he's reduced to one of two things: either a criminal or not-a-criminal. It's a grotesque flattening that deprives him of his more nuanced humanity. And the more prevalent those scenarios are in daily life, the more it deprives us—the rest of the world—of his nuanced humanity and potential contributions. Think of the amount of energy that's put into explaining and defending oneself that could be put toward something else.

In his essay "Autobiographical Notes," James Baldwin says, "I have not written about being a Negro at such length because I expect that to be my only subject, but only because it was the gate I had to unlock before I could hope to write about anything else."[72]

We want to feel as though we stand apart, that we're not subject to the same institutional forces of racism and sexism and classism that have shaped others. We want to have the freedom to write our own stories.

Of course, I'm selfishly pleased that Baldwin produced such exceptional work on being a black, queer man in America, but I wonder, too, what else he might have written if he hadn't felt obligated to reckon with the topic. What other masterpieces might he have produced—what other joys might he have found—if he hadn't felt the all-consuming need to defend his right to a full and free existence?

Right now, putting the more complex narratives of who we are into the world is a matter of survival; it's a necessary counterbalance to the attacks on our capabilities and existences.

I understand why, growing up, I wasn't trying to locate my power and strength in my brownness and femaleness. To accept those terms can cause us to lose out—on job opportunities, on the comfort of a situation. Of course, for some people, the stakes are higher. In many parts of the country, to be openly transgender or gay might still put your life at risk. (Though even on this count, we're starting to see some encouraging shifts: in November 2017 elections across the country, eight transgender Americans were elected into office in states from Georgia to Pennsylvania.[73]) But for many of us, the cost of *not* identifying with the "we"—of sacrificing ourselves on the altar of "I"—is higher in terms of reinforcing a system that keeps screwing us over by denying us true equality and justice.

What if we stopped trying to "look past" the specificities of our experience and identities? Censoring these aspects of our selves coronates people like Lilla, and more dyed-in-the-wool bigots like Sessions, with precisely the crown they seek: "American" as shorthand for "white maleness." White maleness as the origin point, the source of alleged objectivity and neutrality.

What power might we discover by not laundering or censoring our narratives, by undermining this notion that there is some purity of objectivity that we should all aspire to? What powerful vision of a truly egalitarian democracy will *we all* discover by finding common cause with the majority of marginalized Americans?

TAKING BACK
OUR NARRATIVES

REGULARLY TEACH STORYTELLING TO HIGH school students. After a few weeks of brainstorming and practicing, they each perform a story from their lives in front of classmates and friends. It's instructive to see teenagers navigate balancing the truth of their stories with the awareness of how that truth might be received by their peers. One young woman that I worked with wanted to tell a story of self-acceptance: of recognizing that she was more introverted than some of her friends, and making peace with that realization. An important part of her story was relating the experience of losing a friend of hers to suicide—a friend who had gone to the same school she was currently attending.

During dress rehearsal, she hesitated midway through her story, right when she began to describe her close relationship with the friend she had lost. I thought at first it was too emotional for her, and reminded her that she only needed to tell the parts of the story that she felt comfortable sharing. She bowed her head and quietly came over to talk to me: *I'm afraid they won't believe me,* she said, her brows knitted in concern. *What won't they believe?* I asked. *That that's what he was like. That that's what our relationship was like.*

She was afraid, in other words, that her narrative would not be accepted because it wouldn't be recognizable to anyone else. I told her that this was precisely the beauty of her perspective: there is no objective version. Indeed, the only reason her story existed is because it was rooted in her subjectivity and experience. This perspective was a gift—a thread that, added to the memories that other people had of that same friend—created a stronger tapestry, a truer representative likeness of who her friend was.

There's a magic to focusing less on responding to expectations. It breaks a spell which is perhaps simply the myth that we should all fall into one or two particular categories—that our lives and stories must fit a mold in order to be legible to others. But it's the specificity of our identities and experiences that command the ears and hearts of each other. Human beings are incredible bullshit detectors, and listening to someone try to tell a story or truth that is not their own strikes us on a gut level.

Watching that young woman take the stage and tell her story was an experience that drove home how powerful we are when we fully inhabit our stories and our selves: She was soft-spoken at the microphone, which only motivated everyone in the audience to lean in, their bodies listing toward her. Apart from her voice, the silence in the room was absolute. We were all under the spell, watching her claim the role of protagonist in her own story.

Like that young woman, hesitating to tell her story, we learn early on to adapt our narratives based on the people in the room. How much of myself can I share? At what point will what I share become ammunition used against me? So we soften our particularities—and as soon as we do, we give something up.

Watching that young woman perform, I was reminded of the way Baldwin struggled—on the page and in real life—with this question of how to push past expectations to reclaim your self and story. In a 1961 interview, Baldwin tells Studs Terkel:

> All you are ever told in this country about being black is that it is a terrible, terrible thing to be. Now, in order to survive this, you have to really dig down into yourself and re-create yourself, really, according to no image which yet exists in America. You have to impose, in fact—this may sound very strange—you have to decide who you are, and force the world to deal with you, not with its idea of you.[74]

Part of what I've always loved about Baldwin is his ongoing commitment to complicating the conversation about the "race debate." There are times where, listening to recordings of him debating folks, I've wondered at the way he seems to meander so far beyond the terms of the question at hand yet keep you utterly transfixed.

In his 1965 debate with Buckley, Baldwin is asked: "Is the American Dream at the expense of the American Negro?" Baldwin opens by reframing the terms, referring to the question as "hideously loaded, and that one's reaction to that question has to depend on where you find yourself in the world. What your sense of reality ist." He then pivots, saying, "I have to speak as one of the people who have been most attacked by what we must now here call the Western or the European system of reality."[75]

What you're watching is Baldwin repeatedly refusing the narrative in the question as it's constructed. He refuses to abstract his personal experience, to strip his narrative so that it would be more objective or palatable—in line with the way Buckley would like to discuss the "politics" of the "Negro question." He understands that there is no politics without the person, and that it was the fact of his complex selfhood that was already inherently the most political prospect on the table.

Here, then, is a model for how to push back: By surfacing missing narratives that give us a history that more accurately captures our power. By digging more deeply into our own narratives and reclaiming the complexity of them. By no longer walking the tightrope of fulfilling expectations. By refusing the single reductive option offered us, and demanding another one entirely. By acknowledging the realities of the world we're in, and, in the same breath, insisting that another one is not only possible, but necessary.

CONCLUSION

ON A COLD FEBRUARY MORNING in Brooklyn, I followed directions to an old building in Bushwick. I knew I'd reached my destination when I saw an open door, a chalkboard with an arrow pointing the way inside. Up three flights of stairs and into a large room with creaky wood floors, I found a large circle of metal folding chairs. Over the next fifteen minutes or so, people continued to file in. There were communal bagels and coffee, people rubbing the sleep from their eyes, hugs shared between some who knew each other.

By the time the meeting started, there were roughly forty of us there. It was about two months after the election, and an activist friend of mine had invited me along. The goal of the gathering was to discuss taking action to rally Americans in response to the election of Trump. We wanted to come up with a direct action—likely the occupation of some kind of public space—that was engaging and easily replicable in different cities. Something to tap into the rage and fear that so many of us across the country were feeling. Many of the people in that room had robust activism backgrounds—they'd helped coordinate the World Trade Organization protests in Seattle and the 2003 march against the Iraq War in New York City, some were at the heart of OWS organizing.

As someone who has historically identified more as a writer and observer than as an activist, I felt a little out of place. But I was here for a reason: I had felt the sense of utter powerlessness that came from years of covering George W. Bush's presidency, the erosion of truth by those in the highest office of power, the parallel sense of hopelessness and cynicism that blossomed among Americans in response. I did not want to feel that sense of powerlessness again, so here I was on a Saturday morning, drinking tepid coffee at an hour when I would usually still be fast asleep.

That first meeting gave me a powerful sense of hope. After a few hours of initial conversation and planning, we had all committed to going in on an action. We wanted to help spur a people's movement to push Trump—and any other politician who used bigotry to divide Americans and consolidate power and wealth to the 1 percent—out of power.

By the time I left that meeting, I felt like I had found a new home and a new purpose. The rage and fear that had been accumulating in the lead-up to and immediate aftermath of the election now had focus and direction. The plan was to reconvene after doing some legwork in the respective committees we'd broken ourselves into (logistics, messaging, etc.). Over the next couple of weeks, we participated in a frenzy of shared documents and conference calls. We were all working toward the same goal, and it felt like a lifeline, a thread connecting me to some sense of control in a world that felt profoundly chaotic.

PART OF THE CHAOS of my world, too, was that I was falling in love. It seemed like an absurd footnote to the gravity of what was going on politically, but there it was. I had met S. just weeks after the election, and just days before he up and moved to Nashville. What followed were a series of letters and postcards, obscenely long phone calls, and an unspoken mutual commitment to not addressing what it was we thought we were doing by exchanging these growing intimacies from our separate life trajectories.

In January, I bought a plane ticket to Nashville, told S. I would be in town and "maybe we could grab a drink" when I was there. There was literally no other reason for me to be in Nashville except to see S. But as a human being in my thirties who had weathered enough disappointing relationships to have grown cynical about expectations, I had learned to hold my cards close to my chest. I figured I'd see him in person and suss out whether there was something substantive enough there to justify how much real estate he'd come to take up in my heart and mind. Worst case scenario: I'd discover that he didn't reciprocate my feelings and I'd have a fun solo adventure in a city I'd never visited before.

I had that worst-case scenario all wrong. The four days I spent in Nashville were some of the most terrifying of my life. Because S. was far more than I had bargained for. Because I discovered that most of the tools I had to navigate my vulnerability were actually designed to defend and protect against it. They had prepared me for a very particular situation: dating people who didn't value or accept me, or people who simply weren't a good match. What I did not possess were the experience and tools to be in a relationship with a person worthy of my love and openness. The following months—in which S. moved back to New York and we rented an apartment together—had me feeling profoundly out of my depth. I was quick to assume the worst intentions, quick to assume that S. must not care for me as deeply as I did for him. My energies were often put toward parsing things he said to me, evaluating them for evidence that he would inevitably disappoint me.

I can still remember the moment when, in an argument in which I felt slighted, assuming he had deliberately done something unkind, he disarmed me with his pain. I expected him to be defensive or even cruel. Instead, with tears in his eyes, he told me, "It hurts so much that you'd think I would *want* to hurt you."

I wish I could say that this was the last time S. and I had an argument like this, but it's not. Time and again, I watched myself push S. away when I should have pulled him close. Our arguments often ended with me apologizing, weeping, embarrassed. "I'm sorry," I say like a mantra. "I'm so bad at this." S. once asked me early on regarding our relationship: "What do you want this to look like?" I realized I had not truly allowed myself this question. I did not know how to answer it in terms apart from what I knew I *didn't* want it to look like. I knew how to fight, to defend, but I had far less experience with growing, building, envisioning, collaborating.

I wanted this relationship, but I realized that to build it, I would have to work harder than I ever had to create new narratives that could sustain me—and us. And that demanded of me that I reopen a kind of hope that was extremely painful to reckon with.

BACK IN BROOKLYN, OUR protest crew's weekly meetings had reached a serious stumbling block. By March, we all continued to be as passionate about taking action, but—when it came to constructing the platform statement that would be shared publicly—we couldn't agree on language for explaining why we were taking action and what we wanted. We already had an action planned—to occupy a well-known building—and most of us were willing to face arrest in the process. But we couldn't move forward because we couldn't agree on the damn statement. There was a valid and broadly supported argument made for not framing our platform as a "return" to equality and democratic values, since this state has always ever been aspirational. We cannot return to a state that we've never inhabited.

But after hours of discussion and debate, we kept coming back around to two sticking points: Should we center this around a call for Trump to resign? If we did, we'd be taking advantage of a lot of momentum against him, but we all knew that Trump wasn't the only problem. The problem was the system that had allowed someone like him to rise to power. The other sticking point was whether to put words like "Americans," "America," and "democracy" at the core of our message. For some, the words had been too corrupted to lay claim to any longer.

Over a series of Saturday mornings that stretched into afternoons, we debated the parameters of "we"—we in the room wondered who "we" represented and who we were addressing.

It's easy to write this kind of conversation off as navel-gazing, but this question is at the heart of all political action and therefore the heart of all potential political change. Successful movements and initiatives often position this question of "we" at the top. That's true of Marshall Ganz's approach—a celebrated organizer who worked with Cesar Chavez to successfully rally agricultural workers in California and whose grassroots organizing strategy was the linchpin in Barack Obama's 2008 presidential campaign.

As organizer Eric Liu puts it:

> [Ganz] teaches organizers . . . to start not with . . . high concepts like justice but with biographies—their own, and those of the people they hope to mobilize . . . That work then flows into the story of us: the collective narratives of challenge, choice, and the purpose that emerge from any community—that, in fact, help define it . . .[1]

Activating that narrative, according to Ganz and Liu, is what makes it possible to connect with a broader "we"—encouraging others to identify with its clarity and urgency. This work, of course, isn't easy. It demands that we bring to the table the issues and identities that give us the fire to stay engaged, take action, to keep the stakes real and immediate. And it demands that we find ways of weaving these motivations with those of others.

What it notably does *not* ask us to do is abandon vital parts of our selves and our stories in order to construct a story of "we."

SADLY, BY THE END of March, our activist group had disbanded— the differing factions gone our separate ways to pursue our own initiatives and actions. I developed a great respect for the solidarity I found in that group, and the kinds of discussions and arguments we engaged in. Even though an action had not come out of it, it felt like we were doing vital work. I forged friendships in that room that continue to bear fruit.

Yet I'm still haunted by what might have been. I believe a significant obstacle to constructing a powerful "we" came down to a stubborn attachment to our powerlessness and marginalization. We were afraid to use the words "American" and "democracy" because of the way those terms have historically excluded— or been used against—us. But I felt strongly, too, that another reason we were afraid to use them was because of what it might demand of us: to take responsibility for them, to own them, to dictate their terms, and then fight for them.

WE NEED NEW NARRATIVES for our power, and these narratives demand that we reopen our sense of what is possible, what is pragmatic, what is necessary.

Trump and his Chinese-manufactured hats emblazoned with "Make America Great Again" are only the continuation of a long history of exclusionary definitions of "American" being wielded like a weapon against us.

But we're also living in a moment where these terms have never seemed riper for reclaiming.

Around the time that our activist meetings started to fall apart, a "bodega strike" was held, led by Yemeni-American store owners. American flags peppered the plaza in front of Borough Hall, Brooklyn, as thousands of primarily Muslim bodega owners gathered with supporters, prayed publicly, and chanted "USA" in opposition to Trump's immigration ban.[2] Through this simple visual spectacle, they asserted that Trump (and those whose ears had perked to the white-supremacist dog-whistling that pervaded his campaign) could not lay claim to that flag and what it represented.

Here was evidence that we could elbow back, taking ownership of redefining America and democracy. We could complicate the narratives of what they both might mean by insisting on our inclusion. Those bodega owners were holding America to its promise to be a land of welcome, opportunity, and equality. The power in their action came from its clarity and simplicity: they were simply taking these promises, and the symbolism underlying them, at face value rather than assuming a cynical or defeatist attitude. At a time when citizenship and "Americanness" are being policed more heavily than they have in decades, they pushed back with an earnest and vital presumption: America—and the flag representing it—belonged to them as much as to anyone else in this country.

There is power in insisting upon the promises our founders and framers made: Elizabeth Cady Stanton's "Declaration of Sentiments and Grievances" in 1848 helped launch the women's suffrage movement. That document was modeled on the Declaration of Independence—the first four paragraphs almost verbatim— with the pointed inclusion of "women" in certain passages:[3]

We hold these truths to be self-evident: that all men *and women* are created equal.

When I chose to subtitle this book "Claiming Our Power in a Post-Truth America," and throughout when I use the word "we," it is this prefigurative use of "our" and "we" I am thinking of. It's a "we" that encompasses those of us who already identify as marginalized Americans, as well as all of those Americans we will welcome into the fold as they recognize that there is simply not enough oxygen or livelihood in an America dependent on a "we" of exclusion.

TRUMP IS NOT OUR ailment. He is a symptom of it.

As we push forward, we should be skeptical of anyone who

argues that getting rid of Trump will solve our problems, or that we should drop our commitment to "other issues" in order to "unite" under a partisan banner to get rid of him. We are seeing remarkable strides being made in the progressive world—both movements and rising politicians who were inspired to run, or to take a more principled stance after the 2016 election. This is evident in Bernie Sanders's movement for universal health care, and in to the younger voices behind the Congressional Progressive Caucus pushing for green jobs and raising the minimum wage. The politicians who will have the most staying power are those listening closely to the groundswell of grassroots movements— Occupy Wall Street, Black Lives Matter, Fight for $15, climate change, immigrant rights, the student movement to end gun violence—that have never been more vocal and more organized. Where "grassroots mobilization" once commonly meant mobilizing more Americans to vote, it's now moved beyond that meaning to include mobilizing more Americans to run for office.

It's not just Trump and Republicans who are on notice. It's *anyone* in power who fails to heed us. As activist and writer Robert Borosage presciently wrote in *The Nation* in the weeks after the election:

> As the fight against Trump escalates, DINOs—
> Democrats in name only—will face greater pressure
> from these activists, and perhaps primary challenges as
> well. Much of the party's establishment, backed by some
> very deep pockets, will decry these efforts as divisive in
> the face of what they see as Trump's unifying threat.
> This is a denial as purblind as Trump's denial of climate
> change. Democrats need to fight, but they need to fight
> for something, not just against the barbarians. They need

to be the party of fundamental change, not the party of restoration. For that to happen, the activist base of the party has to challenge sitting officeholders not simply to stiffen their opposition to Trump, but to get with the program.[4]

The #metoo movement has become a new thread to strengthen the tapestry of voices united against those who would argue that a successful politics requires us to drop our "personal" issues in the interests of winning. We've seen politicians forced to resign, and we've seen redoubled efforts from Trump to discredit women who have spoken out about sexual violence and harassment. This isn't surprising given that Trump himself faces numerous allegations of sexual harassment and abuse.

It's time to once again own the fact that our personal issues are as political as they come. As writer Laurie Penny put it: "There is a consistent overlap between administrations that laugh off the concept of sexual consent and administrations that see the consent of the governed, too, as a technicality: to be worked around or worn down until they get what they believe they deserve."[5]

When my colleagues and I came together years after working with each other to talk about our abusive former boss, we realized how we had allowed a cartoonish and conveniently narrow understanding of assault and harassment to dismiss our tangible, first-hand experiences of abuse. Where some had been explicitly sexually harassed by him, there were many of us—including myself—who were more subtly manipulated and treated abusively. What we realized when we all came together was how these behaviors and episodes existed along a spectrum, all within a strategic framework. Whether they were sexual in nature or not, they had one thing in common: the unchecked abuse of power.

Entitled white men, including the likes of Donald Trump and Harvey Weinstein, have never paused to question the power that has fallen into their hands; they've never hesitated to claim that all the privileges and freedom symbolized and promised by the American flag and democracy are for them.

Perhaps it's time for those of us who have historically been marginalized to take a page from their books. As writer Sarah Hagi famously said: "God give me the confidence of a mediocre white dude."

What if we laid claim to America and the American flag? It has always been the queerest and brownest among us who have borne the greatest burden of inequality and violence in our country; it is often they who have fought the hardest for gains that benefit all of us. By this measure, the American flag should be the banner of the queerest and brownest among us.

RIGHT NOW, SO MANY of the narratives we've been offered no longer make sense. What does it mean for black, brown, queer, and female Americans to be labeled "marginalized" when we constitute the majority of the population? What does it mean to call our country a meritocracy or democracy when it is all too evident that there are different Americas—different likelihoods of being heard, different degrees of access to success, different systems of education (and incarceration), and even different basic standards of health and well-being—depending on what you look like or how you identify? What does it mean to call our financial system a "free market" when it's rigged with countless mechanisms that allow those with the most wealth to continue to amass ever greater sums while more than 40 million Americans live in poverty?[6]

It's time to make way for new—more accurate—stories.

When accusations of sexual assault and harassment were leveled against Kevin Spacey, Netflix responded swiftly, axing him from the popular series *House of Cards*, which was built around his character—ironically that of president of the United States. Now, the protagonist of the show will be his wife, the first lady. Jeffrey Tambor's star role on the TV show *Transparent* was similarly cut after allegations of sexual harassment emerged.[7] The narratives of these stories must literally be rewritten to focus on other characters.

What happens when the white men who have been our protagonists for so long are sidelined? What other stories will take center stage?

MY FRIEND E., WHO works in the male-dominated tech industry, recently told me that she's implemented a new method whenever men interrupt her at meetings: she keeps talking. "What happens?" I asked. She shrugged. "It's really awkward. I'll keep talking and so do they, and it can go on sometimes for almost a full minute. But I just keep talking, and eventually, they shut up."

It's a small and simple thing, but it struck me as a brilliant, small-scale protest that puts the discomfort back on those who are causing it by insisting on a reality wherein we have the same right to be heard. So many of us do the work daily of minimizing our own comfort and feelings in order to protect the comfort and feelings of those more privileged. What would it look like to collectively refuse to do this any longer? What would it look like to minimize the voices of those who try to minimize us?

In Wunsiedel, Germany, the town has come together to try to put a stop to the neo-Nazis who make an annual pilgrimage to visit the grave of one of Hitler's deputies. They tried exhuming the body and removing the grave stone, but the Nazis still came. So in 2014, they tried a new approach: mockery. Stencils on the street marked the "starting line" of the route as though it were a marathon—not far off base given that residents and businesses pledged to donate money to anti-right-wing extremist groups for every meter the Nazis marched. Locals dressed in clown outfits flank the route, tossing colorful confetti and holding absurd signs.[8]

Protesters across the United States from Seattle to Charlotte have taken a page from their book. Dressed as clowns, they deliberately misunderstood "white power" chants, holding signs that read "wife power" and throwing white flour at neo-Nazi and white supremacist rallies.[9]

As one of the protest coordinators at a Charlotte rally put it: "The message from us is, 'You look silly. We're dressed like clowns, and you're the ones that look funny.'"[10]

There's something deeply compelling about this approach: paying attention—but refusing to listen—to bigots. We do not need to counter every bigoted statement by investing our energy in engaging with the arguments. We need only heed racist figures inasmuch as we need to know what they're up to in order to gauge our safety and to come together to drown them out. Building community by raising our voices together—and having fun in the process—is the added bonus to strategically ignoring those who think they can talk, or wield power, over us.

The #metoo movement has made clear the force of our power when we unite. All of our experiences are unique and uniquely mark us, but together, they speak of a broader problem that we are now demanding be not only acknowledged, but addressed.

It's true that this is exhausting work. In some respects, it's easier to abandon the notion that the world can be different, because a new world means hoping for more, and acting on that hope. It means holding people accountable. It means risking vulnerability, and at times, safety.

It means not opting for the easy and cynical out in which we shrug and say, "I'm not surprised." It means, as Martin Luther King, Jr., called for in 1963 speech, practicing the art of maladjustment:

> Certainly we all want to live well-adjusted lives in order
> to avoid neurotic and schizophrenic personalities. But I
> must say to you . . . that there are some things in my own
> nation, and there are some things in the world, to which I
> am proud to be maladjusted and to which I call upon all
> men of goodwill to be maladjusted until the good society
> is realized . . . And through such maladjustment, we will
> be able to emerge from the long and desolate midnight of
> man's inhumanity to man into the bright and glittering
> daybreak of freedom and justice.[11]

The responsibility of this work falls on all of us, including those who have the power to shape the national consciousness—and inspire action—with their narratives: Comedians and satirists who have the national stage must question whether they're mirroring the same kind of cynicism as those they're intending to satirize. Journalists must examine the subtext of the "objectivity" and "neutrality" that they practice. Recall that in 2013, the Associated Press (AP) made a decision to stop using the word "illegal" in conjunction with "immigrant" because people cannot be innately illegal; rather, it's the legal system that determines whether or not their status is "legal."[12] And the parameters of "legality"—just like "pragmatism" and "common sense"—are constantly shifting.

When Occupy Wall Street was still in full swing, I was working on a story about the role that unions played in the movement. I ended up in conversation with a former union leader in New York, Bill Henning. I was trying to find out what kinds of union strikes might be considered legal or illegal. I was getting frustrated, because he kept ignoring the framework of my question. He wanted to talk about power instead. "Law reflects power relations," he said. "Law gets passed because of power relations. And laws get enforced because of power relations."[13]

It was an important reminder: history shows us that laws do not change unless we demand that they do. I'm hopeful that we can elevate a new generation of political leaders that will reflect new narratives and visions for how the world must be. I'm hopeful that a fiercer journalism—one that acknowledges its role as a vital pillar of our democracy, one that follows a bottom-up reporting reflective of the American people it is working for—will continue to blossom. I'm hopeful our political comedians and satirists will continue moving closer to a kind of humor that puts truth-telling at its center.

But if the immediate aftermath of the 2016 election has taught us anything, it's that we can't rely on those in power to offer us new narratives and visions of what must be. We have to cultivate our own, and work to make them a reality. A huge part of that is asking the big questions—the robustly "naive" questions—What kind of life might offer me the most fulfillment, happiness, and freedom? In what ways does the society I live in make it harder for me to achieve these things? In what ways can I change that?

It's the work of rigorous honesty and self-examination, and the work of bridging the gap between those truths and the expectations we have for our political system.

Activist Eric Liu writes that, if we're being honest and self-critical,

[W]e would have to admit that we haven't really tried democracy yet . . . We haven't truly enabled all the people of this society to participate in self-government to the fullest extent of their potential. We haven't come close, not in an age when our elected officials and their staffs are overwhelmingly white, male, and affluent . . . Not when 48 percent of the new jobs in the country are low-wage jobs paying less than $15 an hour . . . Not when voter turnout is rarely above 60 percent (at best) and when poor, nonwhite, or immigrant voters are still being disenfranchised. What would it look like if we truly were trying?[14]

S. ONCE TOLD ME that he's seen me hesitate to use the word "we" in reference to our relationship. He was right. It's a way in which I've held myself apart, a finger on the button to the escape hatch. But it's a false sense of safety—a cynical posture that bets on the odds of the relationship not working out. It might not. But a real way of ensuring that it doesn't is to continue to keep my finger on that button.

I'm settling into my life with S., which is another way of saying that I'm adapting to being continually maladjusted and uncomfortable. To constantly being reminded of the ways in which I want more but rarely know the language for how to ask for it. To failing S. and being failed by him. To recognizing that I don't yet have all the tools to build the thing I want. But I'm learning as I go. We're learning as we go.

It is a painful hoping, a kind of hope that takes all my courage and bravery. It strikes me that most of us recognize that our personal relationships require constant work. There's a similar daily work that's required of us in our relationship to our country, too. But we're not as familiar with this language in the context of the political realm. The promises built into the fabric of the United States have been betrayed time and again, but we betray these promises, too, by assuming that they can't or won't ever be delivered upon, that we don't play a vital role in bringing these promises to fruition.

The movements we've seen coming together in the Women's March and in the protests that are occurring every day around the country, the roughly six thousand chapters of local activist groups that have blossomed under the "Indivisible" umbrella, are not only a response to the demands of the moment.[15] They are making their own demands that we renew our responsibility and relationship to the country that must be. They are the beginning of a new kind of politics that centralizes the role of the personal. We will need to keep at it long after Trump is deposed and reduced to a troubling chapter in our history books. The work now is writing the chapters that come next, built on our visions founded on a fierce hope, an aggressive "we" that demands of leaders current and future that they heed those in power: Us.

ENDNOTES

1   Martin Luther King, Jr., "Remaining Awake Through a Great Revolution," speech delivered at the National Cathedral, Washington, D.C., March 31, 1968: https://kinginstitute.stanford.edu/king-papers/publications/knock-midnight-inspiration-great-sermons-reverend-martin-luther-king-jr-10.

INTRODUCTION

1   Walt Whitman, *Complete Prose Works* (Philadelphia: David McKay, 1892), 229.
2   Charles C. Mann, *1491* (New York: Alfred P. Knopf, 2005), 94.
3   Ibid., 19, 40, 199.
4   "Historian Says '12 Years' is a Story the Nation Must Remember," by Terry Gross, *Fresh Air*, NPR, October 24, 2013: https://www.npr.org/templates/transcript/transcript.php? storyId=240491318.
5   John Bresnahan, "Bachmann calls for 'penetrating expose' on 'anti-Americans' in Congress," *Politico*, October 17, 2008: https://www.politico.com/blogspolitico-now/2008/10/bachmann-calls-for-penetrating-expose-on-anti-americans-incongress-013248.

6   Barack Obama, speech delivered in Chicago, Illinois, November 4, 2008: http://edition.cnn.com/2008/POLITICS/11/04/obama.transcript/.

7   John McCain, speech delivered in Phoenix, Arizona, November 4, 2008: https://www.npr.org/templates/story/story.php?storyId=96631784.

8   Hamdan Azhar, "2016 vs. 2012: How Trump's Win and Clinton's Votes Stack Up To Romney and Obama," *Forbes*, December 29, 2016: https://www.forbes.com/sites/realspin/2016/12/29/2016-vs-2012-how-trumps-win-and-clintons-votes-stack-up-to-obama-and-romney/#48d1d0ea1661.

9   David Paul Kuhn, "Exit Polls: How Obama Won," *Politico*, November 5, 2008: https://www.politico.com/story/2008/11/exit-polls-how-obama-won-015297.

10 Ron Suskind, "Faith, Certainty, and the Presidency of George W. Bush," *The New York Times Magazine*, October 17, 2004: http://www.nytimes.com/2004/10/17/magazine/faith-certainty-and-the-presidency-of-george-w-bush.html.

11 Robert Dallek, "Power and the Presidency, From Kennedy to Obama," *Smithsonian*, January 2011: https://www.smithsonianmag.com/history/power-and-the-presidency-from-kennedy-to-obama-75335897/#Li7QT4gahVdaSBBF.99.

12 Gregory Krieg, "14 of Trump's Most Outrageous 'Birther' Claims—Half from After 2011," CNN, September 16, 2016: http://www.cnn.com/2016/09/09/politics/donald-trump-birther/index.html.

13 Jonathan Mahler and Matt Flegenheimer, "What Donald Trump Learned From Joseph McCarthy's Right-Hand Man," *The New York Times*, June 20, 2016: https://www.nytimes.com/2016/06/21/us/politics/donald-trump-roy-cohn.html.

14 Grant Smith and Daniel Trotta, "U.S. hate crimes up 20 percent in 2016 fueled by election campaign," *Reuters*, March 13, 2017: https://www.reuters.com/article/us-usa-crime-hate/u-s-hate-crimes-up-20-percent-in-2016-fueled-by-election-campaign-report-idUSKBN16L0BO.

15 Daniel Lombroso and Yoni Appelbaum, "'Hail Trump!': White Nationalists Salute the President-Elect," *The Atlantic Monthly*, November 21, 2016: https://www.theatlantic.com/politics/archive/2016/11/richard-spencer-speech-npi/508379/.

16 Max Greenwood, "Trump tweets: The media is the 'enemy of the American people,'" *The Hill*, February 17, 2017: http://thehill.com/homenews/administration/320168-trump-the-media-is-the-enemy-of-the-american-people.

17 Hillary Clinton, speech delivered in New York City, New York, November 9, 2016: https://www.nytimes.com/video/us/politics/100000004758615/hillary-clinton-concession-speech-highlights.html.

18 Barack Obama, speech delivered from the White House, Washington, D.C., November 9, 2016: https://www.washingtonpost.com/news/the-fix/wp/2016/11/09/transcript-president-obamas-remarks-on-donald-trumps-election/?utm_term=.47372840b0a5.

19 Peter Dreier, "Most Americans Are Liberal Even If They Don't Know It," *The American Prospect*, November 10, 2017: http://prospect.org/article/most-americans-are-liberal-even-if-they-don%E2%80%99t-know-it.

20 Noam Chomsky, *Optimism Over Despair* (Chicago: Haymarket Books, 2017), 116.

21 Eric Zorn, "Ronald Reaganon Medicare, Circa 1961. President Rhetoric or Familiar Alarmist Claptrap?" *Chicago Tribune*, September 2, 2009: http://blogs.chicagotribune.com/news_columnists_ezorn/2009/09/ronald-reagan-on-medicare-circa-1961-prescient-rhetoric-or-familiar-alarmist-claptrap-.html.

22   Michael Regan, "What Does Voter Turnout Tell Us About the 2016 Election?" *PBS News Hour*, November 20, 2016: https://www.pbs.org/newshour/politics/voter -turnout-2016-elections.

23   Sarah Begley, "Hillary Clinton Leads by 2.8 Million in Final Popular Vote Count," *Time*, December 20, 2016: http://time.com/4608555/hillary-clinton -popular-vote-final/.

24   Frank Newport, "Americans Continue to Shift Left on Key Moral Issues," Gallup, May 26, 2015: http://news.gallup.com/poll/183413/americans-continue -shift-left-key-moral-issues.aspx.

25   Ibid.

26   Dennis Loy Johnson and Valerie Merians, eds., *What We Do Now: Standing Up for Your Values in Trump's America* (Brooklyn: Melville House, 2017), 140.

27   Onnesha Roychoudhuri, "How to Take Action—and Stay Sane—in the Trump Era," *Rolling Stone*, January 23, 2017: https://www.rollingstone.com/politics/features /how-to-take-action-and-stay-sane-in-the-trump-era-w462512/.

28   Nia-Malika Henderson, "White men are 31 percent of the American population. They hold 65 percent of all elected offices," *The Washington Post*, October 8, 2014: https://www.washingtonpost.com/news/the-fix/wp/2014/10/08/65-percent-of-all -american-elected-officials-are-white-men/?utm_term=.9d9e7928b6eb.

ON CYNICISM

1   Eric Idle, *The Aristocrats* (New York City: ThinkFilm, 2005).

2   Page duBois, *Slaves and Other Objects* (Chicago: University of Chicago Press, 2003), 155.

3   Daniel Politi, "Women's March on Washington Was Three Times Larger than Inauguration," *Slate*, January 22, 2017: http://www.slate.com/blogs/the_slatest /2017/01/22/women_s_march_on_washington_was_three_times_larger_than _inauguration.html.

4   Scott Malone, Ginger Gibson, "Women Lead Unprecedented Worldwide Mass Protests Against Trump," *Reuters*, Janary 21, 2017: https://www.reuters.com /article/us-usa-trump-women/women-lead-unprecedented-worldwide-mass-protests -against-trump-idUSKBN15608K.

5   Kevin Liptak, "Reality Check: Sean Spicer Hits the Media Over Crowds," CNN, January 21, 2017: http://www.cnn.com/2017/01/21/politics/sean-spicer-fact-check/index.html.

6   Scott McClellan, White House Press Briefing, January 18, 2006: https://georgew bush-whitehouse.archives.gov/news/releases/2006/01/20060118-5.html.

7   Julia Ioffe, "When Protest Fails," *The Atlantic Monthly*, January 21, 2017: https: //www.theatlantic.com/international/archive/2017/01/womens-march-protest -trump-russia/514064/.

8   Shikha Dalmia, "Why the Women's March on Washington Has Already Failed," *The Week*, January 2, 2017: http://theweek.com/articles/667163/why-womens -march-washington-already-failed.

9   Nian Hu, "How the Women's March Failed Women," *The Harvard Crimson*, February 16, 2017: http://www.thecrimson.com/column/femme-fatale/article/2017/2/16/hu -womens-march/.

10 Nicki Rossoll, "Kellyanne Conway 'Didn't See the Point' to Women's March on Washington," ABC News, January 22, 2017: http://abcnews.go.com/Politics/kelly anne-conway-didnt-point-womens-march-washington/story?id=44968455.

11   Elahe Izadi, "Black Lives Matter and America's Long History of Resisting Civil Rights Protesters," *The Washington Post*, April 19, 2016: https://www.washington post.com/news/the-fix/wp/2016/04/19/black-lives-matters-and-americas-long -history-of-resisting-civil-rights-protesters/?utm_term=.5a8cdb8cedef.

12   Paul Herrnson and Kathleen Weldon, "Going Too Far: The American Public's Atti- tudes Toward Protest Movements," *The Huffington Post*, October 22, 2014: https://www .huffingtonpost.com/paul-herrnson/going-too-far-the-america_b_6029998.html.

13   Elahe Izadi, "Black Lives Matter and America's Long History of Resisting Civil Rights Protesters," *The Washington Post*, April 19, 2016: https://www.washingtonpost .com/news/the-fix/wp/2016/04/19/black-lives-matters-and-americas-long-history -of-resisting -civil-rights-protesters/?utm_term=.5a8cdb8cedef.

14   Gal Beckerman, "Getting It Right On Rosa Parks," *Columbia Journalism Review*, October 25, 2005: https://archives.cjr.org/behind_the_news/getting_it_right_on _rosa_parks.php.

15   Valerie Jarrett, "Honoring Rosa Parks on the 100th Anniversary of her Birth," White House Archives, February 4, 2013: https://obamawhitehouse.archives.gov /blog/2013/02/04/rosa-parks-stamp; Paul Schmitz, "How Change Happens: The Real Story of Mrs. Rosa Parks & The Montgomery Bus Boycott," *The Huffington Post*, December 1, 2014: https://www.huffingtonpost.com/paul-schmitz/how-change -happens-the-re_b_6237544.htm

16   Janell Ross, "Rosa Parks Is the Name You Know. Claudette Colvin Is a Name You Probably Should," *The Washington Post*, December 1, 2015: https://www.washington post.com/news/the-fix/wp/2015/12/01/rosa-parks-the-name-you-know-claudette -colvin-the-one-too-many-dont/?utm_term=.0635a17639d0.

17   Brooks Barnes, "From Footnote to Fame in Civil Rights History," *The New York Times*, November 25, 2009: http://www.nytimes.com/2009/11/26/books/26colvin .html.

18   Eric Westervelt, "Act Up In Anger," *Rolling Stone*, April 17, 2017: https://www.npr .org/2017/04/17/522726303/act-up-at-30-reinvigorated-for-trump-fight.

19   Eric Liu, *You're More Powerful Than You Think: A Citizen's Guide to Making Change Happen* (New York: Public Affairs Books, 2017), 111. Liu's book is full of examples of contemporary movements—many of them small- or medium-sized—making re- markable policy strides.

20   Chris Nichols, "Do Millennials Have 'Only a 50-50 Chance' of Doing Better Fi- nancially Than Their Parents?" *PolitiFact California*, October 27, 2017: http://www .politifact.com/california/statements/2017/oct/27/delaine-eastin/do-millennials -have-only-50-50-chance-doing-better/.

21   Martin Luther King, Jr., "Letter from a Birmingham Jail [King, Jr.]," April 16, 1963: https://www.africa.upenn.edu/Articles_Gen/Letter_Birmingham.html.

22   For more on expressive and instrumental actions, visit the Beautiful Trouble website: http://beautifultrouble.org/theory/expressive-and-instrumental-actions/.

23   Andrew Boyd, "Prefigurative Intervention," *Beautiful Trouble: A Toolbox for the Rev- olution*, April 2012: http://beautifultrouble.org/tactic/prefigurative-intervention/.

24   Morgan Whitaker, "Back in the Day: What Critics Said About King's Speech in 1963," MSNBC, October 3, 2013: http://www.msnbc.com/msnbc/back-the-day -what-critics-said-about-king.

25   "Recording Discovered of First Time Martin Luther King Jr. Said 'I Have a Dream'",

Chicago Tribune, August 11, 2015: http://chicagotribune.com/news/nationworld/ct
-mlk-i-have-a-dream-speech-recording-20150811-story.html.

26 Martin Luther King, Jr., speech delivered at the March on Washington, August
28, 1963: https://kinginstitute.stanford.edu/king-papers/documents/i-have-dream
-address-delivered-march-washington-jobs-and-freedom.

27 L.A. Kauffman, *Direct Action: Protest and the Reinvention of American Radicalism*
(New York: Verso Books, 2017), 66–67.

28 "700,000 Female Farmworkers Say They Stand With Hollywood Actors Against
Sexual Assault," *Time*, November 10, 2017: http://time.com/5018813/farmworkers
-solidarity-hollywood-sexual-assault/.

29 L.A. Kauffman, *Direct Action: Protest and the Reinvention of American Radicalism*
(New York: Verso, 2017), 66–67.

30 Ibid., 66–67.

31 Paul L. Montgomery, "Throngs Fill Manhattan to Protest Nuclear Weapons," *The
New York Times*, June 13, 1982: https://www.nytimes.com/1982/06/13/world
/throngs-fill-manhattan-to-protest-nuclear-weapons.html?pagewanted=all; Duncan
Meisel, "Can We Save Our Planet? What the Climate Movement Can Learn
From the Nuclear Freeze Campaign," *Yes! Magazine*, June 1, 2015: http://www.yes
magazine.org/planet/can-we-save-our-planet-what-the-climate-movement-can
-learn-from-the-nuclear-freeze-campaign.

32 Emma Gray, "The Women's March Inspired Them to Run. Now They're Unseating GOP Men," *The Huffington Post*, November 10, 2017: https://www.huffington
post.com/entry/womens-march-inspired-democrats-unseating-gop-men_us
_5a03099de4b06ff32c94cb55.

33 Jeff Guo, "Why Fox News finally dropped Bill O'Reilly," Vox, April 19, 2017:
https://www.vox.com/policy-and-politics/2017/4/19/15361182/bill-oreilly-fox
-harassment-allegations-fired.

34 Adam Gabbatt, Mark Townsend, and Lisa O'Carroll, "'Occupy' Anti-capitalism
Protests Spread Around the World," *The Guardian*, October 15, 2011: https:
//www.theguardian.com/world/2011/oct/16/occupy-protests-europe-london
-assange.

35 Matthew Cooper, "Poll: Most Americans Support Occupy Wall Street," *The Atlantic
Monthly*, October 19, 2011: https://www.theatlantic.com/politics/archive/2011/10
/poll-most-americans-support-occupy-wall-street/246963/.

36 Andrew Grossman, Alison Fox, and Sean Gardiner, "Wall Street Protesters Evicted from Camp," *The Wall Street Journal*, November 16, 2011: https://www.wsj.com
/articles/SB10001424052970204190504577040563377026378.

37 Wray Herbert, "Why 'Occupy Wall Street' Fizzled," *The Huffington Post*, July 30,
2013: https://www.huffingtonpost.com/wray-herbert/why-occupy-wall-street-fi_b
_3676789.html.

38 Eric Liu, *You're More Powerful Than You Think: A Citizen's Guide to Making Change
Happen* (New York: Public Affairs Books, 2017), 5.

39 Ylan Q. Mui, "Americans Saw Wealth Plummet 40 Percent from 2007 to
2010, Federal Reserve Says," *The Washington Post*, June 11, 2012: https://www
.washingtonpost.com/business/economy/fed-americans-wealth-dropped-40
-percent/2012/06/11/gJQAIIsCVV_story.html?utm_term=.4bfe8a34384c.

40 Jonathan Easley, "Obama Campaign Ties Mitt Romney to Wall Street and

Corporate Greed," *The Hill*, October 18, 2011: http://thehill.com/blogs/ballot-box/presidential-races/188129-obama-campaign-ties-romney-to-wall-street-corporate-greed.

41   Adam Gabbatt, "Bill de Blasio Wins By a Landslide to Become New York City Mayor," *The Guardian*, November 6, 2013: https://www.theguardian.com/world/2013/nov/06/bill-de-blasio-wins-new-york-mayoral-election.

42   Alan Feuer, "Occupy Sandy: A Movement Moves to Relief," *The New York Times*, November 9, 2012: http://www.nytimes.com/2012/11/11/nyregion/where-fema-fell-short-occupy-sandy-was-there.html.

43   Colleen Curry, "Occupy Wall Street Offshoot Has Purchased Nearly $4 Million in Student Debt," *Vice News*, September 19, 2014: https://news.vice.com/article/occupy-wall-street-offshoot-has-purchased-nearly-4-million-in-student-debt; http://rollingjubilee.org/.

44   Adam Gabbatt and Ryan Devereux, "Wall Street Protesters to Occupy Foreclosed Homes," December 6, 2011: https://www.theguardian.com/world/2011/dec/06/occupy-wall-street-occupy-foreclosed-homes.

45   Deepti Hajela and Michael Balsamo, "Measuring Occupy Wall Street's Impact, 5 Years Later," Associated Press, September 17, 2016: https://apnews.com/25e3197ee8bc482cb1da20e14819c2fc.

46   "About Us," Fight for $15: https://fightfor15.org/about-us/.

47   "Medicare for All," on Bernie Sanders's official website: https://berniesanders.com/medicareforall/; Jocelyn Kiley, "Public Support for 'Single Payer' Health Coverage Grows, Driven By Democrats," Pew Research Center, June 23, 2017: http://www.pewresearch.org/fact-tank/2017/06/23/public-support-for-single-payer-health-coverage-grows-driven-by-democrats/.

48   Tamara Keith, "Has Bernie Sanders Pulled Hillary Clinton To the Left?" National Public Radio, April 2, 2016: https://www.npr.org/2016/04/02/472434968/has-bernie-sanders-pulled-hillary-clinton-to-the-left.

49   Michelle Nijhuis, "The Teen-agers Suing Over Climate Change," *The New Yorker*, December 6, 2016: https://www.newyorker.com/tech/elements/the-teen-agers-suing-over-climate-change.

50   Manisha Ganguly, "Children to Sue European Countries Over Climate Change," CNN, October 19, 2017: http://www.cnn.com/2017/10/19/europe/portugal-children-climate-change/index.html.

51   Jake Fuentes, "The Immigration Ban Is a Headfake, and We're Falling for It," *Medium*, January 30, 2017: https://medium.com/@jakefuentes/the-immigration-ban-is-a-headfake-and-were-falling-for-it-b8910e78f0c5.

52   Gallup News, "Party Affiliation": http://news.gallup.com/poll/15370/party-affiliation.aspx.

53   Sean McElwee, "Most Americans Don't Vote in Elections. Here's Why," Al Jazeera America, July 27, 2015 http://america.aljazeera.com/opinions/2015/7/most-americans-dont-vote-in-elections-heres-why.html.

54   George W. S. Trow, *Within the Context of No Context* (New York: Atlantic Monthly Press, 1997), 88.

55   Sonam Sheth, "Evening News Programs Have Spent Just 32 Minutes Covering Policy Issues This Election Year, Report Says," Business Insider, October 27, 2016: http://www.businessinsider.com/evening-news-election-2016-10.

56 Thomas B. Edsall, "As Iowa Nears, Clinton Allies Quietly Raise Obama's Cocaine Use," *The Huffington Post*, March 28, 2008: https://www.huffingtonpost.com /2007/12/11/as-iowa-nears-clinton-all_n_76235.html.

57 Ibid.

58 Josh Katz, "Who Will Be President?" *The New York Times*, November 8, 2017: https: //www.nytimes.com/interactive/2016/upshot/presidential-polls-forecast.html.

59 Manila Ryce, "Regis Philbin Plugs 'Democracy Now!'," Video, AlterNet.org, December 26, 2007, http://www.alternet.org/blogs/mediaculture/71497.

60 Jason Linkins, "Worst. Debate. Ever.," *The Huffington Post*, May 25, 2011: https: //www.huffingtonpost.com/2008/04/worst-debate-ieveri_n_97125.html.

61 Madeleine Brand, "A Debate So Bad, 'Soulja Boy' Is Mad?" NPR, April 18, 2008: https://www.npr.org/templates/story/story.php?storyId=89760885.

62 Jose A. DelReal, "Trump Repeated False Claim He 'Was Totally Against the War in Iraq.' Matt Lauer Didn't Press Him on It," *The Washington Post*, September 7, 2016: https://www.washingtonpost.com/news/post-politics/wp/2016/09/07/trump -repeated-false-claim-he-was-totally-against-the-war-in-iraq-matt-lauer-didnt -press-him-on-it/?utm_term=.2ca16bc973c8.

63 Michael M. Grynbaum, "Matt Lauer Fields Storm of Criticism Over Clinton-Trump Forum," *The New York Times*, September 8, 2016: https://www.nytimes .com/2016/09/08/us/politics/matt-lauer-forum.html.

64 Donald Trump, speech delivered in Phoenix, Arizona, August 22, 2017: http://time .com/4912055/donald-trump-phoenix-arizona-transcript/.

65 Mazella, David, *The Making of Modern Cynicism* (Charlottesville: University of Virginia Press, 2007), 19.

66 Mark Andrejevic, *iSpy: Surveilliance and Power in the Interactive Era* (Lawrence: University Press of Kansas, 2007), 252.

67 Stephen Colbert, speech delivered at the White House Press Correspondents' Dinner in Washington, D.C., April 29, 2006: https://www.youtube.com /watch?v=CWqzLgDc030.

68 Erin Corbett, "Stephen Colbert Gives Antonin Scalia the Most Obscene and Touching Tribute Ever," *Bustle*, February 16, 2016: https://www.bustle .com/articles/142233-stephen-colbert-gives-antonin-scalia-the-most-obscene -touching-tribute-ever.

69 Noam Cohen, "That After-Dinner Speech Remains a Favorite Dish," *The New York Times*, May 22, 2006: http://www.nytimes.com/2006/05/22/business/media /22colbert.html.

70 Jonathan Coe, "Sinking Giggling into the Sea," *London Review of Books*, Vol. 35 No. 14, July 18, 2013, 30–31: https://www.lrb.co.uk/v35/n14/jonathan-coe/sinking -giggling-into-the-sea.

71 Frederic Jameson, *Postmodernism, or, The Cultural Logic of Late Capitalism* (Durham: Duke University Press, 1992), 18.

72 Adam Sternbergh, "Stephen Colbert Has America by the Ballots," *New York*, October 16, 2006: http://nymag.com/news/politics/22322/.

73 Ibid.

74 "They're Trying to Kill Us," *The Daily Show*, Comedy Central, April 8, 2008: http: //www.cc.com/video-clips/xw4ywy/the-daily-show-with-jon-stewart-they-re-trying -to-kill-us.

75 "Weekend Update," *Saturday Night Live*, NBC, August 17, 2017: https://www.you tube.com/watch?v=iVvpXZxXWZU.

76 Peter Hamby and Ed Hornick, "Sarah Palin appears on *Saturday Night Live*,'" CNN, October 19, 2008: http://www.cnn.com/2008/SHOWBIZ/TV/10/18/palin .snl/index.html.

77 Ryan McGee, "How 'SNL' Can Get Its Post-Trump Political Credibility Back," *Rolling Stone*, September 27, 2016: https://www.rollingstone.com/tv/news/how-snl -can-get-its-post-trump-political-credibility-back-w441934.

78 David Sims, "The Embarrassment of Jimmy Fallon," *The Atlantic*, September 16, 2016: https://www.theatlantic.com/entertainment/archive/2016/09/the-embarrassment -of-jimmy-fallon-by-donald-trump/500354/.

79 Sandra Gonzalez, "Sean Spicer Tries to Clean Up His Battered Image With a Surprise Emmy Appearance," CNN, September 24, 2017: http://www.cnn .com/2017/09/17/entertainment/sean-spicer-emmys/index.html.

80 Jonathan Coe, "Sinking Giggling into the Sea," *London Review of Books*, Vol. 35 No. 14, July 18, 2013, 30-31: https://www.lrb.co.uk/v35/n14/jonathan-coe/sinking -giggling-into-the-sea.

81 "Confidence in Institutions," Gallup, http://news.gallup.com/poll/1597/confidence -institutions.aspx; Art Swift, "Americans' Trust in Mass Media Sinks to New Low," Gallup News, September 14, 2016: http://news.gallup.com/poll/195542/americans -trust-mass-media-sinks-new-low.aspx.

82 Adam Sternbergh, "Stephen Colbert Has American by the Ballots," *New York*, October 16, 2006: http://nymag.com/news/politics/22322/.

83 Jonathan Coe, "Sinking Giggling into the Sea," *London Review of Books*, Vol. 35 No. 14, July 18, 2013, 30-31: https://www.lrb.co.uk/v35/n14/jonathan-coe/sinking -giggling-into-the-sea.

84 Maureen Dowd, "Jon Stewart and Stephen Colbert: America's Anchors," *Rolling Stone*, November 16, 2006: https://www.rollingstone.com/tv/news/americas -anchors-20061116.

85 Katharine Q. Seelye, "Colbert's Presidential Bid Ends After a 'No' in South Carolina," *The New York Times*, November 2, 2007: http://www.nytimes.com/2007/11/02 /us/politics/02colbert.html.

86 Ibid.

87 Danny Gallagher, "Jon Stewart's 5 Most Hard-hitting Interviews," *The Week*, February 4, 2013: http://theweek.com/articles/468061/jon-stewarts-5-most-hardhitting-interviews.

88 Samantha Bee, *Full Frontal With Samantha Bee*, TBS, March 8, 2017: https://www .youtube.com/watch?v=zpFB2q_3pJo.

89 Stephen Colbert, *The Late Show With Stephen Colbert*, CBS, February 28, 2017: https://www.youtube.com/watch?v=hezHSFSwa08.

90 Mary Jordan, "When Trump Said That Not Paying Taxes 'Makes Me Smart,' Undecided Voters in N.C. Gasped," *The Washington Post*, September 27, 2016: https://www.washingtonpost.com/politics/a-lean-toward-clinton-among-one -group-of-undecided-north-carolina-voters/2016/09/27/ff271b2e-8469-11e6 -92c2-14b64f3d453f_story.html?utm_term=.32067930c652.

91 David Graham, "Was Trump Fibbing About Buying Politicians Then or Now?" *The Atlantic Monthly*, September 6, 2016: https://www.theatlantic.com/politics/archive /2016/09/trump-buying-politicians/498749/.

92 Thomas Frank, "GOP Corruption? Bring in the Conservatives," *The New York Times*, August 22, 2006: http://www.nytimes.com/2006/08/22/opinion/22frank.html.

93 Paul Lewis, *Cracking Up: American Humor in a Time of Conflict* (Chicago: The University of Chicago Press, 2006), 15.

94 Daniel White, "Donald Trump Tells Crowd to 'Knock the Crap Out Of' Hecklers," *Time*, February 1, 2016: http://time.com/4203094/donald-trump-hecklers/.

95 Jordan Fabian and Jonathan Easley, "Trump Defiant: 'Blame on Both Sides' in Charlottesville," *The Hill*, August 15, 2017: http://thehill.com/homenews /administration /346668-trump-there-were-two-violent-sides-in-charlottesville.

96 Andrew Buncombe, "Nagasaki: Wasteland of War, By the First Western Reporter to Witness It," *The Independent*, June 20, 2005 : http://www.independent .co.uk/news/world/asia/nagasaki-wasteland-of-war-by-the-first-western-reporter -to-witness-it-5346082.html.

97 Anthony Weller, "First into Nagasaki: George Weller's Censored Eyewitness Dispatches on the Atomic Bombing and Japan's POWs," The *Asia-Pacific Journal*, Volume 5, Issue 1, January 2, 2007: http://apjjf.org/-Anthony-Weller/2330/article.html.

98 Ben Terris, "The Trump Campaign's War on Reality Made Me Question What I Saw," *The Washington Post*, November 7, 2016: https://www.washingtonpost.com/postevery thing/wp/2016/11/07/the-trump-campaigns-war-on-reality-made-me-question -what-i-saw/?utm_term=.1060cffd8ec2.

99 Julia Carrie Wong and Sam Levin, "Republican Candidate Charged with Assault After 'Body-slamming' Guardian Reporter," *The Guardian*, May 25, 2017: https: //www.theguardian.com/us-news/2017/may/24/greg-gianforte-bodyslams-reporter -ben-jacobs-montana.

100 Bill Ayers, *Demand the Impossible!: A Radical Manifesto* (Chicago: Haymarket Books, 2016), 6–7.

101 Brooke Gladstone, *The Trouble with Reality: A Rumination on Moral Panic in Our Time* (New York: Workman Publishing, 2017), 63.

On Objectivity

1 Jay Allison, Dan Gediman, John Gregory, and Viki Merrick, eds., *This I Believe: The Personal Philosophies of Remarkable Men and Women* (New York: Henry Holt, 2006), xvii.

2 Muriel Rukeyser, *Out of Silence: Selected Poems* (Evanston: TriQuarterly Books, 2000), xiii.

3 Daniel Victor, "'Access Hollywood' Reminds Trump: 'The Tape Is Very Real'," *The New York Times*, November 28, 2017: https://www.nytimes.com/2017/11/28/us /politics/donald-trump-tape.html.

4 Brooke Gladstone and Josh Neufeld, *The Influencing Machine: Brooke Gladstone on the Media* (New York: W.W. Norton and Company, 2011), 69–70.

5 Ibid., 63.

6 "Donald Trump's *New York Times* Interview: Full Transcript," *The New York Times*, November 23, 2016: https://www.nytimes.com/2016/11/23/us/politics/trump-new -york -times-interview-transcript.html.

7 Larry Buchanan, K. K. Rebecca Lai, and Anjali Singhvi, "(Almost) 100 Days of Page One Headlines About Presidents Trump, Obama and Bush," *The New York Times*, April 27, 2017: https://www.nytimes.com/interactive/2017/04/27/us/politics/100 -days-of-page-one-headlines-donald-trump-new-york-times.html.

8   Dahlia Lithwick, "The New Travel Ban Is an Abomination. Why Have We Stopped Caring?," *Slate*, December 6, 2017: https://slate.com/news-and-politics/2017/12 /the-new-travel-is-an-abomination-why-have-we-stopped-caring.html.

9   Fenit Nirappil, Katie Zezima, and Mark Guarino, "With Trump Travel Ban Stay, Immigrants Scramble to Get Back to U.S.," *The Washington Post*, February 5, 2017: https://www.washingtonpost.com/national/with-trump-travel-ban-stay -immigrants-scramble-to-get-back-to-us/2017/02/05/3806cea6-ebb4-11e6-b4ff -ac2cf509efe5_story.html?utm_term=.736ff8d608b8.

10 "NY Times finally speaks the truth and then quickly changes the headline," Daily Kos, January 17, 2018: https://www.dailykos.com/stories/2018/1/17/1733516 /-NY-Times-finally-speaks-the-truth-and-then-quickly-changes-the-headline ?detail=emaildkre; Thomas Kaplan and Robert Pear, "G.O.P. to Use Children's Health Insurance as Lure for Averting Shutdown," *The New York Times*, January 16, 2018: https://www.nytimes.com/2018/01/16/us/politics/government-shutdown -immigration-childrens-health.html.

11 Ben Terris, "The Trump Campaign's War on Reality Made Me Question What I Saw," *The Washington Post*, November 7, 2016: https://www.washingtonpost.com/postevery thing/wp/2016/11/07/the-trump-campaigns-war-on-reality-made-me-question -what-i-saw/?utm_term=.1060cffd8ec2.

12 Eric Umansky, "How Journalists Need to Begin Imagining the Unimaginable," ProPublica, November 23, 2016: https://www.propublica.org/podcast/how-journalists -need-to-begin-imagining-the-unimaginable.

13 Brooke Gladstone, *The Trouble with Reality: A Rumination on Moral Panic in Our Time* (New York: Workman Publishing, 2017), 34–35.

14 Adam Clark Estes and Dino Grandoni, "Another Public Radio Freelancer Gets the Ax Over Occupy Wall Street," *The Atlantic Monthly*, October 28, 2011: https: //www.theatlantic.com/national/archive/2011/10/another-public-radio-freelancer -gets-ax-over-occupy-wall-street/336168/.

15 Elizabeth Flock, "Occupy Wall Street costs two journalists their jobs," *The Washington Post*, October 28, 2011: https://www.washingtonpost.com/blogs/blogpost/post /occupy-wall-street-costs-two-journalists-their-jobs/2011/10/28/gIQA4NN6PM _blog.html? utm_term=.81e2a1a18741.

16 "The Times Issues Social Media Guidelines for the Newsroom," *The New York Times*, October 13, 2017: https://www.nytimes.com/2017/10/13/reader-center /social-media-guidelines.html.

17 David Uberti, "*The New York Times* Demands Its Freelancers Follow Its Bad Social Media Policy or Risk Being Cut," *The Splinter*, December 8, 2017: https://splinternews.com/the-new-york-times-demands-its-freelancers-follow -its-b-1821124052.

18 Lewis Wallace, "Objectivity is Dead, and I'm Okay With It," *Medium*, January 27, 2017: https://medium.com/@lewispants/objectivity-is-dead-and-im-okay-with-it-7fd2b4b5c58f.

19 Adam Clark Estes and Dino Grandoni, "Another Public Radio Freelancer Gets the Ax Over Occupy Wall Street," *The Atlantic Monthly*, October 28, 2011: https://www.the atlantic.com/national/archive/2011/10/another-public-radio-freelancer-gets-ax-over -occupy-wall-street/336168/.

20 Early English Text Society, *Andrew Boorde's Introduction and Dyetary with Barnes*

in the Defense of the Berde (New York: C. Scribner & Co; Leypoldt & Holt), 1870, 116–17.

21 Nina Totenberg, "Sotomayor Faces Questions on Firefighters Case," NPR, July 14, 2009: https://www.npr.org/templates/story/story.php?storyId=106611651.

22 Maggie Nelson, *The Art of Cruelty: A Reckoning* (New York: W.W. Norton and Company, 2012), 138.

23 Noam Chomsky, *Optimism Over Despair* (Chicago: Haymarket Books, 2017), 51.

24 Fred L. Standley and Louis H. Pratt, eds., *Conversations with James Baldwin* (Jackson: University Press of Mississippi, 1989), 5.

25 Farah Stockman, "Women's March on Washington Opens Contentious Dialogues About Race," *The New York Times*, January 9, 2017: https://www.nytimes.com/2017/01/09/us/womens-march-on-washington-opens-contentious-dialogues-about-race.html.

26 Mark Lilla, "The End of Identity Liberalism," *The New York Times*, November 18, 2016: https://www.nytimes.com/2016/11/20/opinion/sunday/the-end-of-identity-liberalism.html.

27 Deborah Povich, Brandon Roberts, and Mark Mather, "Low-Income Working Families: The Racial/Ethnic Divide," Working Poor Families Project, Winter 2014–2015: http://www.workingpoorfamilies.org/wp-content/uploads/2015/03/WPFP-2015-Report_Racial-Ethnic-Divide.pdf.

28 Mark Lilla, "The End of Identity Liberalism," *The New York Times*, November 18, 2016: https://www.nytimes.com/2016/11/20/opinion/sunday/the-end-of-identity-liberalism.html.

29 Eliza Collins, "Sanders: Not Enough to Say, 'I'm a Woman, Vote for Me,'" *USA Today*, November 21, 2016: https://www.usatoday.com/story/news/politics/onpolitics/2016/11/21/sanders-identity-politics/94221972/.

30 Cristina Marcos, "115th Congress Will Be Most Racially Diverse in History," *The Hill*, November 17, 2016: http://thehill.com/homenews/house/306480-115th-congress-will-be-most-racially-diverse-in-history; Laura Cohn, "The U.S. Made Zero Progress in Adding Women to Congress," *Fortune*, November 10, 2016: http://fortune.com/2016/11/10/election-results-women-in-congress/.

31 "Criminal Justice Fact Sheet," NAACP: http://www.naacp.org/criminal-justice-fact-sheet; Heather Long, "African Americans Are the Only U.S. Racial Group Earning Less Than in 2000," *Los Angeles Times*, December 15, 2017: http://www.latimes.com/business/la-fi-african-american-income-20170915-story.html.

32 Tierney Sneed, "Sessions Can't Say If He Thinks Black Lives Matter Is An 'Extremist Group,'" Talking Points Memo, November 14, 2017: http://talkingpointsmemo.com/muckraker/sessions-black-lives-matter-extremist-group.

33 Monique Judge, "Rep. Karen Bass Ate Jeff Sessions for Lunch and It Was Delicious," The Root, November 15, 2017: https://www.theroot.com/rep-karen-bass-ate-jeff-sessions-for-lunch-and-it-was-1820492488.

34 Alanna Vagianos, "30 Alarming Statistics That Show the Reality of Sexual Violence In America," *The Huffington Post*, April 6, 2017: https://www.huffingtonpost.com/entry/sexual-assault-statistics_us_58e24c14e4b0c777f788d24f.

35 Dawne Vogt, "Research on Women, Trauma and PTSD," US Department

of Veterans Affairs: https://www.ptsd.va.gov/professional/treatment/women /women-trauma-ptsd.asp.

36 Susan Rinkunas, "Why Don't Medical Studies Include Equal Numbers of Men and Women?" *New York*, July 21, 2016: https://www.thecut.com/2016/07/why-most -medical-studies-dont-include-women.html.

37 Roni Caryn Rabin, "The Drug-Dose Gender Gap," *The New York Times*, January 28, 2013: https://well.blogs.nytimes.com/2013/01/28/the-drug-dose-gender-gap/.

38 Suzanne Goldenberg, "Why Women Are Poor at Science, by Harvard President," *The Guardian*, January 18, 2005: https://www.theguardian.com/science/2005 /jan/18/educationsgendergap.genderissues; Rebecca Solnit, *The Mother of All Questions* (Chicago: Haymarket Books, 2017), 53.

39 John Sullivan, Reis Thebault, Julie Tate, and Jennifer Jenkins, "Number of Fatal Shootings by Police Is Nearly Identical to Last Year," *The Washington Post*, July 1, 2017: https://www.washingtonpost.com/investigations/number-of-fatal-shootings -by-police-is-nearly-identical-to-last-year/2017/07/01/98726cc6-5b5f-11e7-9fc6 -c7ef4bc58d13_story.html?utm_term=.66cc071e7ec4.

40 L.A. Kauffman, *Direct Action: Protest and the Reinvention of American Radicalism* (New York: Verso Books, 2017), 181.

41 Michael Edison Hayden, Catherine Thorbecke, and Evan Simon, "At Least 2,000 Veterans Arrive at Standing Rock to Protest Dakota Pipeline," ABC News, December 4, 2016: http://abcnews.go.com/US/2000-veterans-arrive-standing-rock -protest-dakota-pipeline/story?id=43964136.

42 Robinson Meyer, "Trump's Dakota Access Pipeline Memo: What We Know Right Now," *The Atlantic Monthly*, January 24, 2017: https://www.theatlantic.com/science /archive/2017/01/trumps-dakota-access-pipeline-memo-what-we-know-right -now/514271/.

43 Naomi Klein, *No Is Not Enough: Resisting Trump's Shock Politics and Winning the World We Need* (Chicago: Haymarket Books, 2017), 227.

44 L.A. Kauffman, *Direct Action: Protest and the Reinvention of American Radicalism* (New York: Verso Books, 2017), 111.

45 Onnesha Roychoudhuri, "How to Take Action—and Stay Sane—in the Trump Era," *Rolling Stone*, January 23, 2017: https://www.rollingstone.com/politics /features/how-to-take-action-and-stay-sane-in-the-trump-era-w462512.

46 Kathryn Schulz, "The Many Lives of Pauli Murray," *The New Yorker*, April 17, 2017: https://www.newyorker.com/magazine/2017/04/17/the-many-lives-of-pauli -murray.

47 Editor Barbara Smith, *Home Girls: A Black Feminist Anthology* (New Brunswick: Rutgers University Press, 2000), 264.

48 Cherríe Moraga and Gloria Anzaldúa, eds., *This Bridge Called My Back: Writings by Radical Women of Color*, 4th ed. (Albany: SUNY Press, 2015), 95.

49 Lindsey Cook, "Why Black Americans Die Younger," *US News and World Report*, January 5, 2015: https://www.usnews.com/news/blogs/data-mine/2015 /01/05/black-americans-have-fewer-years-to-live-heres-why.

50 Sophia Kerby, "The Top 10 Most Startling Facts About People of Color and Criminal Justice in the United States," Center for American Progress, March 13, 2012: https://www.americanprogress.org/issues/race/news/2012/03/13/11351/the-top

-10-most-startling-facts-about-people-of-color-and-criminal-justice-in-the-united -states/.

51 "Violence Against Trans People," Amnesty International: https://www.amnesty usa.org/pdfs/toolkit_transviolence.pdf.

52 Lydia O'Connor, "The Wage Gap: Terrible for All Women, Even Worse for Women of Color," *The Huffington Post*, April 12, 2016: https://www.huffingtonpost.com /entry/wage-gap-women-of-color_us_570beab6e4b0836057a1d98a.

53 Jason Stanley, "Beyond Lying: Donald Trump's Authoritarian Reality," *The New York Times*, November 4, 2016: https://www.nytimes.com/2016/11/05/opinion /beyond-lying-donald-trumps-authoritarian-reality.html.

54 Kevin Liptak and Dan Merica, "Trump Says He Believes Putin's Election Meddling Denials," CNN, November 14, 2017: http://www.cnn.com/2017/11/11/politics /president-donald-trump-vladimir-putin-election-meddling/index.html.

55 Bella DePaulo, "I Study Liars. I've Never Seen One Like Donald Trump," *Chicago Tribune*, December 8, 2017: http://www.chicagotribune.com/news/opinion /commentary/ct-donald-trump-liar-20171208-story.html.

56 Joel Whitebook, "Trump's Method, Our Madness," *The New York Times*, March 20, 2017: https://www.nytimes.com/2017/03/20/opinion/trumps-method-our-madness .html.

57 Jodi Kantor and Megan Twohey, "Harvey Weinstein Paid Off Sexual Harassment Accusers for Decades," *The New York Times*, October 5, 2017: https://www.nytimes .com/2017/10/05/us/harvey-weinstein-harassment-allegations.html.

58 Brooks Barnes, "Harvey Weinstein, Fired on Oct. 8, Resigns From Company's Board," *The New York Times*, October 17, 2017: https://www.nytimes.com /2017/10/17/business/media/harvey-weinstein-sexual-harassment.html.

59 Yohana Desta, "Kevin Spacey Is Literally Being Removed from His Next Film," *Vanity Fair*, November 8, 2017: https://www.vanityfair.com/hollywood/2017/11/kevin -spacey-christopher-plummer-ridley-scott-all-the-money-in-the-world.

60 Dave Itzkoff, "Louis C.K. Admits to Sexual Misconduct as Media Companies Cut Ties," *The New York Times*, November 10, 2017: https://www.nytimes .com/2017/11/10/movies/louis-ck-i-love-you-daddy-release-is-canceled.html.

61 "Roy Moore Loses, Sanity Reigns," *The New York Times*, December 12, 2017: https://www.nytimes.com/2017/12/12/opinion/roy-moore-loss-alabama.html.

62 Melena Ryzik, Cara Buckley, and Jodi Kantor, "Louis C.K. Is Accused by 5 Women of Sexual Misconduct," *The New York Times*, November 9, 2017: https://www.ny times.com/2017/11/09/arts/television/louis-ck-sexual-misconduct.html.

63 James Baldwin, *The Price of the Ticket: Collected Nonfiction*, 1948–1985 (New York: St. Martin's Press, 1985), 405.

64 Eileen Myles, *Cool for You: A Novel* (Brooklyn: Soft Skull Press, 2000), 15–16.

65 James Baldwin, *The Price of the Ticket: Collected Nonfiction*, 1948–1985 (New York: St. Martin's Press, 1985), 262.

66 Julia Carpenter, "How Anita Hill Forever Changed the Way We Talk About Sexual Harassment," CNN Money, November 9, 2017: http://money.cnn.com/2017/10/30 /pf/anita-hill-sexual-harassment/index.html.

67 Aaron Blake, "Trump jokes (?) about firing Nikki Haley: 'She could easily be replaced,'" *The Washington Post*, April 24, 2017: https://www.washingtonpost

.com/news/the-fix/wp/2017/04/24/trump-jokes-about-firing-nikki-haley-she-could-easily-be-replaced/?utm_term=.34c63327b230.

68   Susan Chira, "The Women Who Still Like Trump," *The New York Times*, April 29, 2017: https://www.nytimes.com/2017/04/29/sunday-review/the-women-who-still-like-trump.html.

69   Gloria Steinem, *My Life On the Road* (New York: Random House, 2016), 12.

70   Eric Liu, *You're More Powerful Than You Think: A Citizen's Guide to Making Change Happen* (New York: Public Affairs Books, 2017), 32.

71   Molly Ball, "The Short List: No. 2 Person of the Year Donald Trump," *Time*: http://time.com/time-person-of-the-year-2017-donald-trump-runner-up/.

72   James Baldwin, *Notes of a Native Son* (Boston: Beacon Press, 1955), 8.

73   "Meet the Transgender Americans Who Won on Election Day," Human Rights Campaign, November 8, 2017: https://www.hrc.org/blog/meet-the-transgender-americans-who-won-on-election-day.

74   Fred L. Standley and Louis H. Pratt, eds., *Conversations with James Baldwin* (Jackson: University Press of Mississippi, 1989), 5–6.

75   "James Baldwin Debates William F. Buckley," 1965: https://www.youtube.com/watch?v=oFeoS41xe7w

CONCLUSION

1   Eric Liu, *You're More Powerful Than You Think: A Citizen's Guide to Making Change Happen* (New York: Public Affairs Books, 2017), 130.

2   Adam Chandler, "The Yemeni Bodega Strike," *The Atlantic Monthly*, February 4, 2017: https://www.theatlantic.com/business/archive/2017/02/yemen-bodega-brooklyn-immigration-ban/515670/.

3   Eric Liu, *You're More Powerful Than You Think: A Citizen's Guide to Making Change Happen* (New York: Public Affairs Books, 2017), 73.

4   Robert L. Borosage, "Resisting Trump Is Not Enough," *The Nation*, February 16, 2017: https://www.thenation.com/article/beyond-resistance/.

5   Laurie Penny, "The Consent of the Ungoverned," Longreads, December 2017: https://longreads.com/2017/12/05/the-consent-of-the-ungoverned/.

6   Philip Alston, "Extreme Poverty in America: Read the UN Special Monitor's Report," *The Guardian*, December 15, 2017: https://www.theguardian.com/world/2017/dec/15/extreme-poverty-america-un-special-monitor-report.

7   John Koblin, "Amazon Moves On Without 'Transparent' Actor Jeffrey Tambor," *The New York Times*, February 15, 2018: https://www.nytimes.com/2018/02/15/business/media/transparent-jeffrey-tambor-sexual-harassment.html.

8   Moises Velasquez-Manoff, "How to Make Fun of Nazis," *The New York Times*, August 17, 2017: https://www.nytimes.com/2017/08/17/opinion/how-to-make-fun-of-nazis.html.

9   Tina Rosenberg, "Neo-Nazis in Your Streets? Send in the (Coup Clutz) Clowns," *The New York Times*, September 6, 2017: https://www.nytimes.com/2017/09/06/opinion/comedy-protest-taxes-nazis.html.

10   Nick Wing, "White Supremacist Rally In North Carolina Met By Clown Counter-Protest, 'Wife Power' Signs," *The Huffington Post*, November 12, 2012: http://huffingtonpost.com/2012/11/12/white-supremacist-rally-clowns_n_211890.html.

11 "Newly Discovered 1964 MLK Speech on Civil Rights, Segregation and Apartheid South Africa," Democracy Now!, January 5, 2018: https://www.democracynow .org/ 2018/1/15/newly_discovered_1964_mlk_speech_on.

12 Paul Colford, "'Illegal Immigrant' No More," *Associated Press*, April 2, 2013: https: //blog.ap.org/announcements/illegal-immigrant-no-more.

13 Bill Henning, Interview with the author, January 16, 2017.

14 Eric Liu, *You're More Powerful Than You Think: A Citizen's Guide to Making Change Happen* (New York: Public Affairs Books, 2017), 62–63.

15 Karin Kamp, "The Indivisible Movement Is Fueling Resistance to Trump," *Salon*, February 15, 2017: https://www.salon.com/2017/02/15/how-the-indivisible -movement-is-fueling-resistance-to-trump_partner/.

ACKNOWLEDGMENTS

THIS BOOK IS the result of conversations with people far smarter than me to whom I owe an incalculable debt of thanks and gratitude. Any errors between these covers are solely the result of my own oversights or boneheadedness. Thanks to the patience and passion of Emma Paterson at Rogers, Coleridge and White as well as Dennis Johnson, Valerie Merians, Taylor Sperry, Alexandra Primiani, and the rest of the Melville House crew; in praise of Michelle Legro for saving my ass in a very timely manner; thanks to Los Angeles Review of Books, who published the initial essay, "Our Four Years," from which this book sprang; with gratitude to

Ben Strader, Harriet Barlow, and Blue Mountain Center for the gifts of time and home; special thanks to Mikhaela Reid, Renee Dorris, Karina Jougla, and Nadine Ahrabi-Nejad at Doctors Without Borders for their support and flexibility; raising a glass of prosecco to Susan Duprey, whose house was a haven that made so much more possible; love and thanks to my Moth and Speech/Act crew for being generally incredible and reminding me of the moon's impact; in solidarity with and appreciation for my AlterNet crew; huge thanks to friends and colleagues whose stories and suggestions helped shape this book: Eddie Martinez and Andrea Thome, Meehan Crist, Sarah Manyika, Virginia Vitzthum, Michal Lumsden, Deanna Zandt, Bill Floyd, and Esther Ben-Ami; a special shout-out to L.A. Kauffman whose work is an inspiration. Conversations with her, as well as her book *Direct Action: Protest and the Reinvention of American Radicalism*, put meat on the bones of so many of my arguments; love and thanks, as always, to Andrew Boyd for relentless support, storms of the brain variety, and ribbing; love and thanks, too, go to Evan Derkacz, Ryan Greer, Rachel Beider, Alena Graedon, Laughlin Siceloff, Eva Steele-Saccio, Mary Peelen, Ruby Rich, Janice Kang, Sam Eifling, the ladies of Flying V, Mel Evans, Kristina Rizga, Jean Rohe, Liam Robinson, and Lygia Navarro for vital friendship, pudding pudding, apartments, deep-sea factoids, rainforest junkets, angry peaches, whiskey, and other forms of support when I needed it most; thanks to Micaela Blei for Tuesdays, no matter the day of the week; to Julia Harrison (always); for my family: Mai, Baba, Asim, Dee, Nana, Grandpa, Shawn, and Daovy, who have always inspired me to ask the deeper questions; love and gratitude to Courtney Zoffness and Jane Rose Porter for being the fiercest of Vs, and, to Skye Steele: there's no one with whom I'd rather write new stories.